Celebrity and the Media

Key Concerns in Media Studies

Series editor: Andrew Crisell

Within the context of today's global, digital environment, *Key Concerns in Media Studies* addresses themes and concepts that are integral to the study of media. Concisely written by leading academics, the book consider the historical development of these themes and the theories that underpin them, and assess their overall significance, using up-to-date examples and case studies throughout. By giving a clear overview of each topic, the series provides an ideal starting point for all students of modern media.

Published

Paul Bowman   *Culture and the Media*

Andrew Crisell   *Liveness and Recording in the Media*

Tim Dwyer   *Legal and Ethical Issues in the Media*

Gerard Goggin   *New Technologies and the Media*

David Hendy   *Public Service Broadcasting*

Shaun Moores   *Media, Place and Mobility*

Sarah Niblock   *Media Professionalism and Training*

Sean Redmond   *Celebrity and the Media*

Forthcoming

Steve Cross   *Religion and the Media*

Terry Flew and Stuart Cunningham   *Media Economics*

Gerard Goggin and Kathleen Ellis   *Disability and the Media*

Brian McNair   *News Media*

Monika Metykova   *Ethnicity and the Media*

Kate O'Riordan   *Science and the Media*

Niall Richardson and Sadie Wearing   *Gender and the Media*

Sue Turnbull   *Media Audiences*

Celebrity and the Media

Sean Redmond

First published 2014 by PALGRAVE MACMILLAN

Palgrave Macmillan in the UK is an imprint of Macmillan Publishers Limited, registered in England, company number 785998, of Houndmills, Basingstoke, Hampshire RG21 6XS.

Palgrave Macmillan in the US is a division of St Martin's Press LLC, 175 Fifth Avenue, New York, NY 10010.

Palgrave Macmillan is the global academic imprint of the above companies and has companies and representatives throughout the world.

Palgrave® and Macmillan® are registered trademarks in the United States, the United Kingdom, Europe and other countries

ISBN: 978–0–230–29268–0

This book is printed on paper suitable for recycling and made from fully managed and sustained forest sources. Logging, pulping and manufacturing processes are expected to conform to the environmental regulations of the country of origin.

A catalogue record for this book is available from the British Library.

A catalog record for this book is available from the Library of Congress.

Printed in China

To my Father, Peter Redmond, for singing Danny Boy, badly. To my children, Joshua, Caitlin, Erin, Dylan, and Cael, for your wayward ways, and for your refusal to accept the word 'no'. Dance. To Jodi, my love, for giving me the key to exit the loneliness room.

Contents

Acknowledgements

I would like to thank Jodi Sita for thinking through the small and big ideas of this book. In particular, her insightful comments on the metronome allowed me to see and hear it more clearly not only 'out there' in the world made of celebrity, but 'in me', the man made in the image of celebrity culture.

I would like to thank John Downie for the daily car journey conversations that allowed me to understand melancholy more fully, life more easily, and to see myself outside of the loneliness room.

I would like to thank those who discuss celebrity culture with me on a regular basis and whose conversations have impacted on how I see and hear celebrity: Su Holmes, David Marshall, Kim Barbour, Tamara Heaney, and Allison Maplesden.

I would like to thank Craig Batty for so beautifully sensing Zac Efron.

The sections, 'Bieber Fever' and 'The Passion Play' had their first airings as 'blog' items on CSTonline.

1   The Celebrity Metronome

I am on the treadmill at the gym trying to loose fat, increase my muscle, and harden my body like a wrestling Mickey Rourke. In front of me are a row of plasma TV screens all switched to different channels with their sound turned off. On each and every channel there is a celebrity show being aired: Judge Judy, E! News, an action flick starring Bruce Willis, a cable cosmetics show fronted by a television personality I know the face of but not the name, a Rihanna music video, an episode of Two and a Half Men, a local news bulletin anchored by a celebrity journalist, and a replay of a Barcelona soccer game where the demi-god, Lionel Messi, scores a hat-trick.

As I run my eyes switch from one screen to the next, glancing at the row of celebrity figures before me. As my pace quickens, the TV screens take on the enchanted form of a celebrity metronome, my own perception caught in a regular and regulated swing. I see modern life itself griped by the metronome's fixed beat, by the quiet pulse of auratic bodies that fill the swinging screens. I see the celebrity metronome beating across all of time and space, bringing to the world the 'everywhere' of celebrity culture. This I tell myself is the age of the celebrity metronome. And I run more quickly.

I   Will Always Love you

Ask yourself these framing questions about Whitney Houston's death on 11 February 2011:

How did you first hear about her death?
Where did you go to confirm the details, to learn more about the
    tragic event?
Was it through Facebook or Twitter, on a mobile device as you trav-
    elled through town?
How did you respond, who did you talk to, or where did you post
    about her death?

Where did you hear her songs being played and images of her celebrity circulated?

Did her songs sound out on radios, tablets, and mobile phones; in shopping malls; and on music channels, so that her soprano voice seemed to permeate all around you?

Did you follow the outcry that greeted Sony raising the download price of Whitney's anthem, *I Will Always Love You*?

What type of narrative about her life emerged across the media?

How was Bobby Brown portrayed?

Were race, drugs, and religion a core part of the rise-and-fall narrative trajectory employed to define Houston's life and death?

What types of emotional reactions did the media countenance?

Did you feel *moved or manipulated* by the media representation of her death?

Why did she dominate the news, the front pages of magazines, tribute shows, the posts and tweets that rolled off Facebook and Twitter over the period from her death to her funeral?

Why did Whitney Houston's death seem to matter?

For the most part, in answering these questions you will see that Houston encapsulates what celebrity involves, and how it functions like a mechanical metronome moving in and between media platforms, social interactions, and ritualised events, with similar stories, representations, reactions, and emotions being aligned and activated. In a very real sense, Whitney's death is produced, scripted, given a media representation, and is understood to be felt in particular heightened ways by fans and consumers.

Whitney Houston's death might be best described as a concentrated 'flashpoint' event when 'a particular celebrity completely dominates media coverage, producing an excessively focused global public' (Turner, Bonner, and Marshall, 2000: 6). For example, on the day of her death *The Sun* (News international, UK) newspaper led with, 'TROUBLED superstar Whitney Houston was found dead in a hotel room bath after two nights of heavy partying, it has been claimed', while *Fox News* reported, 'Whitney Houston, who reigned as pop music's queen until her majestic voice and regal image were ravaged by drug use, erratic behaviour and a tumultuous marriage to singer Bobby Brown, died Saturday night. She was 48'. Both reports set in motion how Houston's death will be framed and represented: talent and success wrecked by addiction and abuse; a rise-and-fall trajectory that involves the recognition of her greatness followed by grandiosity, wayward diva behaviour and a doomed relationship with a fellow star (Bobby Brown), racially stereotyped as the 'bad buck' of the piece.

Such was the significance given to her death by the media, and such was the concentration by them on fan identification and the subsequent mourning period, that Houston became the centre point of news and current affairs discourse. The coverage focused on personal tragedy, and confessional and affective responses, as it was imagined to have impacted upon Houston, and on the people touched by her death. In fact, at this time one would have had to disconnect from the social world not to have met or perhaps felt Whitney's death so pervasive was the media coverage and the call for common communion.

Celebrity matters because it exists so centrally to the way we communicate and are understood to communicate with one another in the modern world. Celebrity culture involves the transmission of power relations, is connected to identity formation and notions of shared belonging; and it circulates in commercial revenue streams and in an international context where celebrated people are seen not to be bound by national borders or geographical prisms.

The notion of celebrity, of whom might be a celebrity, and of the issues, concerns, and pleasures that it raises are readily accessible to everyday conversation. People willingly give their opinions on celebrity in all sorts of political, social, and domestic contexts. In fact, if one was able to tune one's ear into café and bar conversations, mealtimes at work, playground huddles, radio broadcasts, the chatter of the social media; or if one was to hone one's eyes onto bedroom walls, magazine-filled coffee tables, designer and perfumery shops, all manner of goods and services, and the broad output of television and cinema, then one would find celebrity sounded out and visualised large. And this sounding is like the constant beat of a metronome, and this vision is like its regulated swing.

The material and cultural evidence of celebrity, then, is everywhere to be seen and heard. For example, as of the 30 May 2012, Lady Gaga had 25 million fans (her 'Little Monsters') following her daily tweets. She tweeted: '#25milliontweetymonsters wow! I'm officially feeling like the luckiest girl in the world today'. These little monsters cross age, gender, class, and race boundaries; they come from all four corners of the world; and the interaction with Gaga fulfils significant individual and cultural needs, particularly around the theme of alienation and disenfranchisement since she proclaims that she looks after, and speaks to and for, the marginalised in society.

Celebrity exists at the centre of media and cultural life. It is found in the political arena, the literary circuit, and the boardrooms of big business and software companies. Celebrity is found wherever elevated figures can be foregrounded as heightened, charismatic, and talented people who warrant or demand our attention, and who can speak to or embody the needs, desires, and fears that sit at the core of modern life. The question of what celebrity constitutes is seemingly an easy one to answer and yet beneath its obviousness lays a deeper and more complex set of issues, debates, and dilemmas. This is a monograph dedicated to exploring the vexing but fascinating intricacies of celebrity culture. Journey with me.

What Is Celebrity? I Am (Not) Celebrity

If one was to visit any high street in almost any part of the industrialised world today and asked 'ordinary' people the question, 'what is celebrity', there would be general agreement to the answers given: they are famous people; you see them in films, on the television, on YouTube; and out in public, often at glamorous events. You can read about them online, and in magazines, fanzines, and newspapers. They are often connected to brands, and advertising campaigns, for any number of products and services. A celebrity is someone that for the most part leads a glamorous and wealthy life, and they are especially talented. Or, alternatively, they are undeserving of their fame, simply being well-known for being well-known (Boorstin, 1992). One can watch celebrities perform in their site-specific talent arena such as the concert hall or sports stadium, or at a red carpet entrance on a film's gala opening night. One can follow their lives through biographies and diaries, and in real time, at any time, through the social media. This ubiquity and proximity allows fans to get to intimately know a celebrity and to interact with, and gossip about, them. Celebrities are desirable and desiring; they exist as models of perfection, and yet they are also often damaged, toxic figures that are immoral models of imperfection and consequently are bad for us in some way. There is too much of them, since celebrities dominate the news and as such 'trivialise current affairs' (Gitlin, 1997: 35).

In asking ordinary people what is celebrity, one would undoubtedly reveal that there is a great deal of cultural knowledge about what it constitutes, that it has major political, economic, and cultural ramifications, and that it exists in a sea of contradictions and tensions.

The opinions on celebrity would be proven to swing this way, then that, forming a metronome modulating inside of people, shaping their perception of what the modern world means to them. Everyone has an opinion on celebrity since it is the actual material out of which contemporary life is experienced and understood, for better or for worse.

In academic terms, the term celebrity is used to define a person whose name, image, lifestyle, and opinions carry cultural and economic worth, and who are first and foremost idealised popular media constructions. According to Rein, Kotler, and Stoller, 'a celebrity is a name which once made by the news, now makes news by itself' (1997: 14). Celebrities exist in the eye of the media, are often adored by their fans, and are valuable commodities in terms of their use and exchange value. They are 'idols of consumption' (Lowenthal, 1961), and promote the purchasing of commodities through lifestyle choices and product endorsement.

For example, Charlize Theron is an A-listed Hollywood film star who attracts funding for any film project she is connected with, and in turn has a fan base who will go to see the films that she appears in. After the Oscar-nominated success of *Monster* (Jenkins, 2003), Theron earned $10,000,000 for starring in both *North Country* (Caro, 2005) and *Aeon Flux* (Kusama, 2005). According to *The Hollywood Reporter*'s 2006 list of highest-paid actresses in Hollywood, she ranked seventh, behind Halle Berry, Cameron Diaz, Drew Barrymore, Renée Zellweger, Reese Witherspoon, and Nicole Kidman. The average gross of her films is $28,935,398.

Theron has a pre-constituted star image that suggests certain repeat behaviours and values; she brings to her starring film roles performative promises and these are raised as expectations by the marketing machinery and through the way her fans consume her. At the level of signification, Theron registers as an idealised white female beauty (a blonde bombshell) but she is also represented as feminist and authorial. Theron is both to-be-looked-at and takes on challenging roles and gives authentic, realist performances. She stars in Hollywood blockbusters such as *Hancock* (Berg, 2008), which operate through a desiring gaze of her body, and she takes roles in films such as *North Country* (Caro, 2005), which define her as an activist, fighting injustice and (sexual) harassment.

Theron is readily reported on, her public and private life a constant newsworthy source in the popular media. Again, this is bifurcated coverage. On the one hand her support for and commitment to women's rights, animal welfare, and same-sex marriage is well documented. On the other hand, she is reported on through the lens of sexual objectification and fascination. For example, when her mobile phone was hacked and 'nude' pictures were circulated in 2012, Theron's identity was sexualised even if this was under the mask of media indignation.

In terms of commercial sponsorship, Theron's endorsements centre on products that make use of her beauty and glamour. She advertises Dior perfume (signed 2004), Uniqlo Heattech's designer clothes (signed 2010), and was associated with Raymond Weil's luxurious Swiss watches (2005–2006), appearing in a series of adverts that connected her elegance and beauty with the product in question. For all these global products, Theron is represented to be glamorous, sensual, and, with the Dior brand, particularly sexual.

For the j'adore Dior campaign, in one notable magazine advert, a bronzed Theron emerges from a golden sea, as she strides towards the imagined reader. Her blonde hair is swept back, and wet, and the golden, strapless dress she is wearing reveals her flawless skin. Her hourglass body shape, and the perfected sensuous symmetry of her body, is meant to mirror the perfume, the perfume bottle, which occupies the right corner of the image-advert. Theron is 'made' of it, is found in the perfume's very essence; in this advert there is a shared sexual chemistry constituted as a sexual fantasy enveloping perfume and celebrity.

Theron, then, exists in all the interconnecting sheets that define celebrity, linking identity, desire, gender perfection, emulation, news, gossip, and commodification across the texts and contexts we find her represented in. She is the epitome of a certain *type* of celebrity.

Celebrity Types

According to Chris Rojek (2001), one can divide celebrities into distinctive types. First, there is ascribed celebrity based on lineage and 'whose status typically follows from blood-line' (17). Members of royalty, the aristocracy, and heirs and heiresses have ascribed celebrity status. Second, there is achieved celebrity which 'derives from the perceived accomplishments of the individual in open competition' (18), and which would include film stars, pop stars, sports stars, leading artists, inventors, elite scientists, and grand philanthropists. Third, there is attributed celebrity, which is, 'largely the result of the concentrated representation of an individual as noteworthy or exceptional by cultural intermediaries' (18). Reporters, publicists, photographers, personal trainers, and chat show hosts, amongst others, highlight these attributed individuals because of single acts of bravery, invention, difference, certitude, and honour. Or else, their accumulative extraordinary actions and activities are considered to warrant attention and reporting on. Attributed celebrity can also emerge because of what are considered to be heinous acts and infamous behaviour, such as the atrocities undertaken by a serial killer. Fourth, there is the celetoid, which is 'any form of compressed, concentrated attributed celebrity' (21). For Rojek,

> The desire for fame now far exceeds talent, accomplishment or skill. The upshot of the present condition is the emergence of the *celetoid*: a person who acquires short, intense bursts of media time simply by dint of being recognized by TV producers as coveting and chasing fame in a sufficiently determined way. (2009)

The 'accidental celebrity' (Turner, Bonner, and Marshall, 2000) would also fall into this category of the celetoid. Thrust into the limelight because of an incident or event outside of their control, they become newsworthy for a distinctly limited period of time.

For example, in January 2009, Captain Chesley 'Sully' Sullenberger became an accidental celebrity when he landed US Airways Flight 1549 on the Hudson River after its engine had stalled after hitting a flock of geese on take off. Sully was thrust into the media spotlight and heralded a hero for his successful landing of the aircraft. Stories about his training, his family life, and his American-born 'exceptionalism' dominated the US news outlets, culminating in him being ranked second in *Time* magazine's 'Top 100 Most Influential Heroes and Icons of 2009'. Accidental celebrities are generally ephemeral, the length and reach of their fame limited to the size of the accidental event that first thrusts them into the spotlight.

Questioning Types: Fusion Figures

The idea of celebrity types is, nonetheless, a problematic one, not least because one can argue that celebrities always exist as *blended* constructions where their status and discursive meaning constantly shifts depending on context, event, and media specificity. Prince William has ascribed celebrity status as a member of the British Royal family, and this is particularly represented as such during state ceremonies and official engagements. However, he also has attributed celebrity status in relation to his skills as a flight lieutenant with the Search and Rescue Force. His six-week tour of the Falklands was widely reported in terms of heroic duty. Finally, prior to his marriage to Katy Middleton, Prince William was a regular feature of the tabloid press in terms of his playboy ways and wild partying. He was in effect, in this representational stream, a celetoid. And yet not quite, it is the conjunction of ascribed and attributed status, situated in textual and contextual environments, that render celebrities such as Prince William fusion figures, where ritualised events and specific media sites foreground particular aspects and qualities of the fêted individual in question.

Star Struck

There is also the issue of media and role specificity that complicates the taxonomy of celebrity types. The film, sports, and rock star may well need their own celebrity categories because of the way they signify and are culturally positioned, while the television personality can be understood to be a (domestic) celebrity figure with specific, defining characteristics (Bennett, 2011).

Stars often warrant the greatest attention, attract particularly strong levels of attraction and idolisation, and they exist at the apex of the commercial and commodity revenue streams. Soccer star David Beckham, for example, was named richest UK sportsman in the *Sunday Times* (2012) with earnings of over £160 million. The event-like status attributed to a Beckham appearance positions him as a particularly idolised and famed individual. As Ellis Cashmore suggests

> The Beckham fairy tale ... grew out of this fertile soil, a context in which people had lost trust in established traditional forms of authority, in which they no longer looked to monarchic, military, religious or political leaders for guidance and in which they found gratification in immersing themselves in the lives of glamorous and flamboyant celebs. (2004: 2)

In a similar vein, Chris Rojek suggests that celebrities such as David Beckham 'have filled the absence created by the decay in the popular belief in the divine right of kings, and the death of God' (2001: 13).

Beckham, in fact, has been captured in religious style poses, has a well-publicised tattoo of *Jesus on way to the Cross*, and has undertaken ambassadorial work that allow him to play the role of healer and life-giver.

If we take the example of the contemporary film star, Christine Geraghty has usefully suggested that they can be read in terms of three distinct forms, only one of which is connected to celebrity. First, there is the star-as-celebrity whose fame exists primarily in terms of the reporting of events in their leisure and private life, relegating the films they appear in to secondary significance. As Geraghty argues, 'it is the audience's access to and celebration of intimate information from a variety of texts and sources which are important here' (2007: 101). Second, there is the star-as-professional who has a stable star image that cements itself in film roles that call on similar performance cues, in repeated and recurring ways. Geraghty argues that Harrison Ford is one of the most successful professional stars since 'Ford is absolutely consistent in performance, and enjoyment of a Ford film very much depends on watching the contrast between easy expressiveness of his body movements and the impassive face with its limited range of expressions' (102). Third, there is the star-as-performer who is primarily noted for their acting talent, the skill of their performances, and the work undertaken to make a performance shine. Geraghty says that the recent shift to performance-driven stardom is in response to celebrity culture and to the way cinema has been digitised and ever more reliant on special effects and artifice. The star-as-performer humanises film in the age of simulacra. If one was to take the tragic example of Australian actor Heath Ledger, one can see how the question of authenticity of the performance, the implicit method behind the star figure, was integral to his star signification and the way viewers and fans responded to him. Ledger was understood to be an authentic actor with stardom acting like an albatross around his beautiful neck.

Ordinary Television Personalities

The television personality can arguably be considered to also be a category in its own right. John Ellis has provocatively argued that television presents audiences with a personality or 'someone who is famous for being famous, and is famous only in so far as he or she makes frequent television appearances' (1992: 96). John Langer has suggested that the television personality is a relatively stable identity that emerges in and between the flow of programming and genre segmentation (1981). They should be contrasted with film stars because

> Whereas stars emanate as idealizations or archetypal expressions, to be contemplated, revered, desired and even blatantly imitated, stubbornly standing outside the realms of the familiar and routinized, personalities are distinguished for their representativeness, their typicality, their 'will to ordinariness', to be accepted, normalized, experienced as *familiar*. (1981: 355)

The idea that television personalities are ordinary and attainable, who go by their real names in authentic or realist environments, suggests a particular site-specific category with important ideological and cultural considerations. As James Bennett (2011) argues

> Television personalities must be understood as actively involved in the promotion, and maintenance, of particular meanings about what it means to be 'ordinary' across a range of identity formations: from national identity to race, sexuality to gender. (191)

If one were to examine the *Oprah Winfrey Show* and Winfrey's personality, one would see its logic being tied to the ordinariness of her presentation of the self, one built on stability and familiarity and a high degree of intimacy. The structure of the show, its segments and bridges, its confessional and therapeutic mode of address, and Winfrey's common touch with guests and audience alike suggest a particular interpersonal and dialogic configuration of the television personality. However, wrapped around Winfrey's television persona are the complex markers of race, gender, sexuality, and class since she both embodies and reads or self-reflects on these as part of the show. Invited guests and audience are also asked to comment on them, often for progressive political reasons. Winfrey is very much one of us, she

> [t]ouches audience members a lot, cries and laughs, and they touch, laugh and cry back. These exchanges signify an empathy that is traditionally feminine, but also feminist in its insistence on the 'personal', and that is largely free of the inflections of authority and sexuality mixed in with the male hosts' touching. (Squire, 1994, 66)

Consequently, the way in which the television personality connects with political issues leads one to consider representation and identity as key criteria when considering the way celebrities are to be understood.

Celebrity and Identity

The idea of celebrity types needs nuancing in terms of class, gender, race and ethnicity, and sexuality. The celebrity occupies identity positions through which ideology and power relations are negotiated and articulated. The celebrity type, then, is a blended construction not simply because of fluidity in the way they occupy the stage, but because they are always given multiple identity positions that shape their status.

Serena Williams is a celebrity tennis player; she has achieved this position through skill and fortitude. She is also – depending on the context – a celetoid, written about because of her bad temper, highly defined arm and leg muscles, body weight, and her spending power. As an achieving celetoid she is also decidedly raced and sexualised by the popular media, her African roots used to fetishise her body, particularly her buttocks. As Coleman-Bell suggests

> The media concentration on Williams's buttocks seems to confirm the way that race, gender and sexual deviancy and desire are aligned. Williams's sporting prowess is encoded as a form of sexual excess: she doesn't just play sport, she is sport. The representation of Williams's black sporting body is loaded with carnal connotations so that she becomes a compliant whore for the white imagination that she is centrally 'packaged' for. (2004, 199)

Celebrities are always connected to vexing questions about identity, they 'articulate what it is to be human being in contemporary society; that is, they express the particular notion we hold of the person, of the individual' (Dyer, 1987: 10). The type of individual that gets celebrated however needs to be individuated, they need to be seen to exist as something unique or special, and this is best encapsulated through the way the celebrity body is made to signify, to be the material out of which identities and subjectivities emerge. Such celebrity individuation, however, may open new, challenging, and intimate ways to understand why and how they matter to people.

Celebrity Bodies

Celebrities are always embodied individuals, and one of their key signifying capabilities is communicating through the senses, through sensorial representations. Rather than their being celebrity types, then, one might better express their meaning in terms of celebrity bodies – through their sensorial and corporeal manifestations. Skin, hair, lips, eyes, touch, sweat, movement, arms, legs, and torso are concentrated upon by the visual media, and the senses seem regularly heightened or super sensitivised, ensuring that celebrities are *especially* carnal beings.

From a negative position, the celebrity body may emerge as a particularised sensory stereotype, such as the way Serena Williams has become a modern version of the vivacious Hottentot Venus, a racialised figure used at the turn of the nineteenth century to suggest an innate sexual difference between black women (enlarged labia, buttocks) and white women. By contrast, white female celebrities often are framed as having ideal bodies that are to be attained and attainable to those who work them into pictures of health and slender fitness. These thin, toned, white celebrity bodies are centrally involved in reproducing the 'tyranny of slenderness' (Chernin, 1994) that haunts popular media culture more generally. According to Maltby, Giles, Barber, and McCutcgheon's study of teenagers and adolescents

> Findings suggest that in female adolescents, there is an interaction between Intense-personal celebrity worship and body image between the ages of 14 and 16 years, and some tentative evidence has been found to suggest that this relationship disappears at the onset of adulthood, 17 to 20 years. Results are consistent with those authors who stress the importance of the formation of para-social relationships with media figures, and suggest that para-social relationships with celebrities perceived as having a good body shape may lead to a poor body image in female adolescents. (2005: 17)

There is, however, a more general and positive phenomenological perspective from which to understand the conceit that the celebrity is an embodied figure that needs to be *experienced*; as one that requires a recognition of a level of intimacy or intimate engagement that is not reducible to representation and performance. That is, to engage with the celebrity requires feelings, the activation of the senses, and the mobilisation of affects. For example, I cannot see or hear Bruce Willis without also sensing sweat, physical exertion, movement, and more recently and in synaesthetic contradiction, embodied melancholy and existential inertia – slowness or a slowing of affects as he has aged. One could profitably put together taxonomy of celebrity bodies in terms of sensation and feeling.

Marilyn Monroe (cotton, milk, sugar, softness, water)

When concentrating on celebrity types as a framing taxonomy one also forgets to look at what I would like to term celebrity aesthetics or the ways in which celebrities are made meaningful through aesthetic design and narrative and performative choices; through the techniques of lighting and styling, colour and fabric choice; and through appearing in heightened, utopian environments. Examining the spectacular celebrity body in these enchanted places would reveal something particular about identity and desire, particularly if one was to simultaneously situate the reading in particular historical contexts. For example, Marilyn Monroe's sensorially transmits what it is like to be a perfected white woman in a 1950s America dealing with racial difference. She creates an 'experience' of desirable white womanhood for an America undergoing radical social and political transformation. Her body moves freely, it registers as soft and appealing, the embodiment of girl-like optimism and womanly sensuality; it is full and fecund, but vulnerable and fragile, always in corporeal tension with itself.

Celebrity Aesthetics and the Celebaesthetic Subject

It is through these latter contexts – celebrity embodiment and aesthetics – and in relation to the imagined fan or consumer, that I would like to introduce one new term to the field of celebrity studies, borrowed from Vivian Sobchack's definition of the cinesthetic subject in her book *Carnal Thoughts* (2004). For Sobchack, the cinesthetic subject is the one that 'feels his or her literal body as only one side of an irreducible and dynamic relational structure of reversibility and reciprocity that has as its other side the figural objects of bodily provocation on the screen' (79). As Sobchack explains, the term 'cinesthetic' is meant to comprise the way in which the cinematic experience triggers and relies on both synaesthesia (or intersensoriality) and coenaesthesia (the perception of a person's whole sensorial being).

I think we can usefully define the feeling, sensing subject in front of the star or celebrity as the *celebaesthetic subject*. The fan and celebrity face one another as carnal beings in a dynamic, relational structure of reversibility and reciprocity, through which the senses are activated and the body is the organ through which a communion, a shared experiential relationship, takes place. Put rather simply, stars and fans communicate with one another in and through the activation of powerful emotions and senses. Let me draw on an illustration to help me better explain this.

The Crying Man

Sam Taylor Wood's *Crying Men* series took 20 male Hollywood stars and photographed them crying, emoting, in various intimate settings. One can, of course, apply the lens of artifice, of performance register and star image to these photographs as if they are singularly media representations. The photographs clearly exist in a commodity marketplace where Hollywood careers are being constructed and mythologised. Art, popular culture, and commodification mix and conjoin in these photographs, as does the star artist (Wood) who is the 'auteur' capturing these famed, masculine figures.

In a particularly affecting image of Daniel Craig one can read the emotion he expresses as part of his filmic image. Craig is the James Bond that cried, and there is a certain fragility to his eyes which speak the performative vocabulary of hurt and forlorn melancholy. For me though, as I conjure up my own response to seeing or feeling the photograph for the first time, there is something else about it that, to use Roland Barthes (1982) term, wounded me.

The photograph is beautifully shot; sunlight dances around the loft apartment setting and creates a shadow on Craig's face, and across his somber body. Craig, leaning forward, hand to lower face, is seated in a black leather chair. The foreground of the photograph is predominantly dark and thick. His eyes are red and swollen and bags of exhaustion half circle their raw edges. The image is a mixture of dry and wet; with the sun and the tears acting as affective registers of heat and water, heart and emotional outpouring. The hand that cups the lower face is one that would wipe away the tears or steady the convulsing face. They would be salty and sodden. The image is still but it moves. Craig's hair is messy, roughed up and the stare he returns is directed at the viewer/reader, at the photographer behind the camera. The stare is wrought, confessional, and it exists as intensity that is felt in *this* body, my body, as it experiences the stare in the moment of the first live encounter with it. It heats and floods my emotions. I experience it synaesthetically (as light, elements, colours, tastes) and I see or sense the carnality of the image before me. Craig's physical and emotional self (hard and soft, masculine and homoerotic) scatters itself across the vibrations of the photograph. Little of this is accidental, of course, it is the stadium at work, the photograph's recognizable code, but some of what I experience though may well be crafted out of blocs of sensation and asemiotic registers of feeling.

Craig's pain desires and devours me as it eats away at his own self in the image. But the image or photograph affects me in another elemental way, like a knife through the primordial heart. This is the punctum of the photograph or to quote Barthes, in *Camera Lucida*, 'that accident which pricks me (but also bruises me, is poignant to me)' (1982: 26–27).

What is in this photograph that wounds me so, what object, trace, cloth, or texture resonates in the realm of the senses? I don't see it at first, can't see its point, and the points it leads to. Its significance a buried affect in a sea of melancholy. Then it hits me, it is the thick gold band on his curled finger – missing from my own finger, left in a bathroom dish somewhere, confirming the end of a relationship.

I can immediately feel the coldness of the ring, its absence on my finger. Craig's emoting body provides a synaesthetic and coenaesthesitic symbiosis that takes me over. I/we exist in a dynamic relational structure of reversibility and reciprocity in which my senses are activated and my body is the organ through which communion, a becoming, takes place. Put simply, that is me crying in the picture, a becoming Craig, me crying before the picture, a Craig becoming me, an affecting outcome that can only be put into words now. I am a fan of Craig – there is something for me deeply affecting about his masculinity – and this acts as an opening which allows me to lose and find myself in the crying man series.

Julia Kristeva has suggested that when one attends an art installation it is the body that is being asked to sense the work, but not as an abstraction. Rather, 'one experiences the installation as a real experience that rises out of the encounter with its form, colour, volume, its internal and communicable sensations' (quoted in Bann, 1998: 69).

I would like to suggest that this might be the project or primary function of celebrity aesthetics: to explore the way celebrity activates our intensive registers, and reconnects us in newly profound and perhaps liberating ways with the social world. This aesthetic, sensorial thread and its liberating potential will be one of the recurring frames through which celebrity will be explored in this book.

But where did celebrity come from?

We Shall All Be Kings and Queens: The Rise of Celebrity Culture

How to best make sense of where celebrity began; to navigate how it has charted over human history; and how it is presently constituted? One of the difficulties in doing this genealogy is the ambiguity over terms, or the slight variations in related terms that are so often treated the same way. How might renown and infamy differ from celebrity, for example? Can one discern links or a chain of associative relationships across Western culture with regards to the narratives of celebrity? Are there epochal shifts, and if so why, with what consequences? There are two broad positions; the first speaks of continuities; and the second speaks of historical breaks. I shall now take each of these positions in turn.

Continuities

Renown and fame can be argued to have long histories, with their origins in ancient civilisation. If we look at the Latin root of the term celebrity we see that it derives from the word *celebritās* or multitude, renown, festal celebration, and is equivalent to *celebr-* (stem of *celeber*), or that which is often repeated. Fame, as Robert Garland argues, comes from the 'Latin word fama, cognate with the verb "to speak", an enduring characteristic that outlived a person's demise' (2005: 24). In their original usage both terms link celebrity and fame to public recognition built upon achievement or noteworthy behaviour. The idea that renown is spoken ('to speak') is related to the way notable people would be often discursively positioned to be the voices of reason and sound opinion. Renown occurs not only through oration but the display of wealth and power, and the physical presentation of the self in ritualised and performative settings. The philosopher Socrates, for example, is remembered as a remarkable figure through the way he delivered and presented philosophical truths to disciples and those under his study. The theatre or arena or court became the primary site for renown to be instigated.

However, this speaking sensibly and importantly must occur in front of an audience and be recorded and remembered. For renown to take root it must be written about or sketched; it must be retold in folk story and song; and it must be circulated fully within and across the culture of the time for it to have lasting impression. In these respects, Socrates lives on as a figure of renown because of what others wrote about him, including Plato. On today's terms, publicists, cultural intermediaries, and journalists take a key role in the creation of renown, but this occurs alongside televised recordings, social media interactions, interviews, performances, and the responses from those who witness the celebrity in action.

Socrates is an interesting example to use because of the gaps and contradictions that appear in these writings about both his private and public life. In effect, Socrates embodies the tension that straddles the history of celebrity, in whatever form it takes, between what is imagined or reported to be real and authentic, and what is read to be artifice and construction. Of course, it is these very tensions in the circulation of renown that helps create and sustain the figure as worthy of significance and import. The enigma of Socrates is the fuel for gossip, intrigue, doubt, attraction, and repulsion; it is the crux of celebrity culture today as it was then.

One can suggest, then, that at least on one important level there is a strong link between the birth of renown and contemporary celebrity, and that they fulfil similar human needs. Tom Payne (2010) argues that idols or celebrities emerge because they fulfil both loving and hateful tendencies that all humans possess. The celebrity is to be adored but they are also to be destroyed since this ritual of loving, then hating, and then killing them provides a safe or symbolic space to play out essential and transhistorical desires and death drives. Celebrity is 'a systematic cycle of celebration, consecration and sacrifice' (51) whose ritualised narrative allows one to create immortalised figures that one can then safely destroy. Through identification with the celebrity, one can get to know perfection, and death, at a relative safe distance and without being consumed by either of them.

One of the key narrative arcs of the celebrity figure is the rise-and-fall trajectory. No sooner does the celebrity reach the heights and highs of success than they fall prey to drugs, booze, instability, and a career nosedive (see the discussion of Whitney Houston which heads this chapter). The drama of their rise-and-fall is played out in numerous media outlets, and is again scripted. This might be represented through the way their wayward body is witnessed stumbling out of a club in the early hours, or into limousines or taxis that whisk them away, their faces shielded from public view. This paparazzi shot becomes emblematic (repeatedly circulated) of their fall from grace. Or their decline is evidenced through how ill their bodies are shown to be, and which therefore bear the hallmarks of the slow slide to metaphorical death – the death of their celebrity status – and to a real death that may soon consume them. As consumers, as fans, we revel in the rise-and-fall story; contribute to its circulation; and we only get our full fix if both consecration and desecration takes place.

In terms of media representation, Lindsay Lohan carries the burden of such a trajectory. A notable child star and a Disney Princess, she is seen to fall from grace. As she entered adolescence, it is reported that she has began to drink, take drugs, misbehave, and had a 'lesbian' relationship. This profile of damage is extended and connected to the reports on her having a criminal record for drink driving and for the need for her to enter a rehabilitation clinic. On 14 June, for example, Fox News reports, 'Drug Outbreak behind Lindsay Lohan Rehab Switch, Sources Say' (http://www.foxnews. com/entertainment/2013/06/14/drug-outbreak-behind-lindsay-lo-han-rehab-switch-sources-say/), while Perez Hilton posts, 'Lindsay Lohan Wanted Out Of Betty Ford ASAP, Her "Safety And Sobriety" Were In Danger!!!' (http://perezhilton.com/category/lindsay-lohan#. UbvjsJV_1pE).

Through these sequential, 'further falling down' frames, we watch her innocence fall away, and either take a moral stance, rebuking her, a sympathetic or empathetic line, or we take pleasure in her undoing, and we wait for death to consume her. Of course, the rise-and-fall trajectory for the celebrity can also have a further 'act', one where a resurrection or rebirth takes place, and the celebrity is seen to rise again, having cleaned up their act and learned from past mistakes. Britney Spears would be a celebrity who has risen after falling. This is not yet the case with Lohan. In the 2012 January edition of *Playboy*, Lohan is captured in a nude Marilyn Monroe inspired photo shoot, and she recently played Elizabeth Taylor in the television biopic, *Liz and Dick* (Lifetime, 2012). Lohan is reanimating herself in the bodies of dead stars who themselves had turbulent lives. Death envelops her present celebrity status.

Epochal Shifts and the Death of the Real

Nonetheless, rather than seeing continuities, a number of scholars suggest that there are epochal shifts in the history of celebrity. Fred Inglis, for example, sees a clear shift between fame and the development of celebrity in the eighteenth century in Europe and North America. For Inglis, fame is based on birth, wealth, skill, and power while one can become a celebrity by 'the mere fact of a person's being popularly acknowledged, familiarly recognized, attended to, selected as a topic for gossip, speculation, emulation, envy, and groundless affection' (2010: 57). Inglis argues that first the Enlightenment, and then the Romantic period and the Industrial Revolution, paved the way for celebrity culture to emerge since it set in motion a number of massive transformations that re-shaped modern life. This included the rise of the cult of the individual; the development of consumerism, fashion, new leisure, and entertainment streams; the rise of the popular press, the invention of cinema; and a philosophical turn to emotion which favoured feeling, desire, and passion over rational choices and rationalist paradigms.

For Inglis, London, Paris, and New York are the key cities in this enabling of modern fame, and Lord Byron the epitome of the shift to the celebrated individual since he embodied its new modes of address. Byron was written about in gossip-centred newspaper columns and his life became a work of art to be celebrated. For Clara Tuite, Byron heralds in the age of literary celebrity and with it new modes of production and communication between writers and readers

> a figure distinguishable from the merely famous author by his or her status as a cultural commodity produced by highly-developed capitalist relations of production and consumption and a fully industrialized form of print capitalism. With the rapid expansion of literary markets from the late eighteenth century, works of literature were no longer produced for a small audience, often known to the author, but for a vast, anonymous body known as the reading public. With the emergence of the public, a radically altered relationship between writers and readers created the conditions for the culture and economy of literary celebrity, which overcame this distance and established an intimacy between the author and reading public. (2007: 62–63)

In relation to Bryon, this intimacy manifested itself in the way romantic love was both writ large across his oeuvre, and was carried into his very public relationship with Carloline Lamb, rendering it 'a form of publicity' (Tuite, 2007: 62), and as a way of offering access to his most intimate desires, feelings, and wants. One can see a relationship between this literary, romantic intimacy, and the modern forms that are carried by celebrities in the social media, and by emotional outpourings in confessional contexts such as the television chat show.

Inglis sees some cultural benefit to the age of celebrity since it can provide social cohesion and collective meaning. However, he also sees a rapid decline in the worth of celebrity over the course of the twentieth century, since it becomes devalued, an empty vessel that now operates at the level of spectacle and capitalist consumption. Daniel Boorstin takes up a similar position when he suggests

> The hero was distinguished by his achievement, the celebrity by his image. The celebrity is a person well known for his well-knownness. We risk being the first people in history to have been able to make their illusions so vivid, so persuasive, so realistic that we can live in them. (1992; 49)

Boorstin argues that we live in the age of the 'pseudo-event', manufactured by the media, organised around mythical events of importance and which take the place of, or stand in for, social reality. For Boorstin, we live in and through banal media representations only, and the celebrity is the epitome of the 'human pseudo event' since they are 'fabricated on purpose to satisfy our exaggerated expectation of human greatness' (ibid.).

Mark Rowland is even more critical of contemporary celebrity culture, again locating a rupture from the Enlightenment period onwards, out of which, 'new variant fame' or vfame emerges, a state in which 'we are constitutionally incapable of distinguishing quality from bullshit' (2008: 91). For Rowland, vfame is akin to disease, or mental illness, and consequently Western culture is similarly contaminated by it and has undergone a 'severe dementia' (26). Vfame is a symptom of a Western world where Britney Spears can be considered to be 'just as good as Beethoven' (103), but where in truth such comparisons are 'truly facile' (104). In fact, Rowland considers that cultural relativism has lead to a state in which ordinary people can no longer make critical sense of their lives, too busy are they with consuming empty celebrity signifiers and comparing the merits of, say, *Hello!* magazine with the *E!* entertainment channel.

One can posit an alternative argument about contemporary celebrity, however: one that contextualises criticisms of it in terms of a nostalgia for a past that never really existed, and which sees it in terms of a greater democratisation of access to media representations and discourses. For example, Leo Braudy argues

> The longing for old standards of 'true' fame reflect a feeling of loss and nostalgia for a mythical world where communal support for

achievement could flourish. But in such societies that did exist, it was always only certain social groups who had an exclusive right to call the tunes of glory, and other visual verbal media were in the hands of a few. (1986: 585)

Graeme Turner identifies what he terms the demotic turn in celebrity culture which involves the 'increasing visibility of the "ordinary person" as they have turned themselves into media content through celebrity culture, reality TV, DIY web-sites, talk radio and the like' (2010: 2). For Turner this demotic turn has contradictory outcomes. On the one hand, increased participation in the media doesn't necessarily correlate with increased power and authority. On the other hand, it does ensure a visibility and a centring of themes and issues not hitherto given media oxygenation.

There is a concern that the superficiality of celebrity activity reduces the opportunity for meaningful political participation for ordinary people as the media centre gets filled with the trivial, the neo-liberal, and the late capitalist dreaming that stands in the way of critical, public engagement. In Stuart Hall's recently released *The Kilburn Manifesto* (2013), he suggests that celebrity is at the cultural heart of the development of the possessive and aspirational individualist, concerned with self-development as it can develop within or through the engines of late capitalism. Hall contends

Neoliberalism's victory has depended on the boldness and ambition of global capital, on its confidence that it can now govern not just the economy but also the whole of social life. On the back of a revamped liberal political and economic theory, its champions have constructed a vision and a new common sense that have permeated society. Market forces have begun to model institutional life and press deeply into our private lives, as well as dominating political discourse. They have shaped a popular culture that extols celebrity and success and promotes values of private gain and possessive individualism. They have thoroughly undermined the redistributive egalitarian consensus that underpinned the welfare state, with painful consequences for socially vulnerable groups such as women, old people, the young and ethnic minorities.

But this may not be the case, in fact, there is good evidence to suggest contrary impulses and connections can and does occur through celebrity culture. Joke Hermes (1995), for example, has examined the pleasure that women readers get from gossip magazines that are often heavily centered on celebrity news. She found that readers used gossip for two productive reasons; first, as an extended family through which items could be shared; and second, as a melodrama, that could be related back to everyday life. Both reasons gave readers a collective and inclusive environment to talk through the issues facing them. Gossip about celebrities, then, is considered to be a powerful tool to engage with the serious issues that women faced in their everyday lives. It has feminine and feminist possibilities that counter the patriarchal way that public discourse is often shared and communicated.

The rise of the social media may also be a productive instrument in the way celebrities interact and are interacted with today. Celebrities can emerge outside of the corporate streams they very often are connected to, and the communal groups that emerge around a celebrity can directly impact upon the way that celebrity negotiates their fame and public presentation. The social media have produced a much more fluid environment for the circulation of celebrity figures and so power and authority are clearly no longer able to be transferred from top to down, but in new carceral networks that allow them to flow in irregular and new ways. Similarly, celebrities can use the social media for activist reasons, aiming to bring a political issue into the spotlight and produce collective momentum in trying to change it. As *The Guardian* reported,

> Josie Long (32,214 followers), a stand-up comedian who supports the UK Uncut movement, finds Twitter an essential forum for debate. 'I do feel chuffed that I've got that many people on my Twitter, and I can disseminate things', she says. 'I feel quite proud that I'm letting people know about protests and actions and things like that'. (Benedictus, 2011)

Politicians of course have increasingly turned to the social media to launch their campaigns and to develop electable profiles, particularly with young voters. The co-mingling of celebrity qualities with political standing has begun to shape politics on a global scale. As I have elsewhere written (2010), Obama used the social media to connect with and mobilise his vote, employing his slogans of change and hope within the context of media technologies and media content that were built on change and hope metaphors. This alignment was particularly attractive, offering a synergy between the needs of the individual, social media organisations, and users who embraced Obama's mantra of social change.

The Celebrity Metronome

I would like to make one final comment on the here and now of celebrity. First, the modern media enable us to consume a celebrity outside of any linear order. Through the processes of media convergence, media portability and mobility, and time shifting in television-viewing habits and the simultaneous erosion of time-driven schedules, a celebrity's past and present can be watched or read or viewed in any number of sequences, in any order a fan so wishes. A celebrity's past and present can be re-ordered and with it the ideological weight that may have sat with them at any given particular time. As their own linear relationship to time is unlocked, so is their capacity to simply stand for an ideological position.

Age and the ageing process becomes something quite different in this unhinged multi-versant universe. The rise-and-fall celebrity trajectories previously addressed in this chapter and which are often used to mark a celebrity's career path can no longer have the linear certainty that they might have once had. A celebrity's body can seem to co-exist in different physical states, and they can be re-animated, brought back to life through the digital hologram, as Tupac was for the 2012 Coachella musical festival. Celebrities not only live beyond death through the recycling of their image, works, but in and through a digital media that can constantly return us to their living present. In this respect, Lohan is the epitome of this recycling and re-examination process. One can access all points of her career at any one time, she can fall before she can rise again as a child star; and we can pull pieces from this bricolage and foreground what is most important to us.

Celebrities are liquid figures because time can no longer be theirs, or their cultural intermediaries, to hold firm. They exist across numerous temporal and spatial dimensions. I can watch Charlie Sheen in one half-hour segment of *Two and Half Men* looking younger than he does in the next, out of sequence, half-hour segment that immediately follows. This can be then be 'interrupted' by Ashton Kruchtner performing the role. I could Google Sheen and see him appear in 20 different simultaneous states and go to old tweets where he was still married or expressing that he was in madly love with a 'hooker'. I can be given the task of archivist to give his life order but I may very well allow or be compelled to allow the collapse of time to match my own experience of modern life liquid – transient, ephemeral, fluid, cut up, and mixed.

Celebrity now embodies the condition of liquid modernity – it presents us with figures to identify with but asks us to see or experience these embodied ties as loose, free-floating. And yet not quite, liquid celebrity is contained within a meta-framework, held in the power of a mechanical device that regulates and governs its waters. This is the celebrity metronome, sounding out, swinging its single hand, over everything that exists in the world today.

Zac Efron (deep blue ocean, sculpted marble, musky, Earl Grey tea, smooth and solid).

2 Seeing the Celebrity Image

I look in the bedroom mirror and see Mickey Rourke staring back. He is the Rourke who starred in Diner: *thin, young and strong. I feel good about myself, staring at Mickey staring back. When I blink and look again he has changed. He looks like a wrestler, beaten up, weathered, but nonetheless proud. When I blink again it is just I looking at myself in the mirror, imagining I was Mickey Rourke performing in* Diner.

Seeing Celebrity Everywhere

In the modern world the image is everywhere to be seen. The world is a visual canvas made up of spaces, objects, devices, pictures, photographs, videos, and regulatory signs that require us to orientate ourselves visually. The way we see the world is organised through a range of vision machines and spatial schemata that enable us to look all around, and to search or gaze into things deeply. Whether this be through high-powered optical devices, surveillance cameras, smart mobile phones; or through the way the exteriors of shops are designed to look into, or their interiors are designed to look around, we are asked to orientate ourselves as seeing beings first.

Vision is increasingly mobilised through digital technologies that can render the image free from its indexical root, allowing us to see things that were never physically there in the first place, including our own presence, if we so wish. We can Photoshop our bodies into any event we would like to be seen in, including a red carpet entrance with a favourite celebrity. Seeing and been seen takes place in a visual culture or

[t]he existence of particular structures for the gaze, for seeing and for the excitement, desire, voyeurism or fear in looking; visual culture always provides a physical and psychical place for individual spectators to inhabit. (Evans and Hall, 1999: 4)

The onset of the Industrial Age heralded this modern turn to all things visual and with it the vision, the image, of the celebrity. They exist at the centre point of a world organised around the pleasure (and terror) of looking. Celebrity culture is vision orientated, crafted out of rituals, events, texts, products, and encounters that are organised around the ocular and the haptic, since our eyes are very often calibrated as organs of touch. The seeing of the celebrity activates desires and identifications, physical sensations within us, and the celebrity often reciprocates this desiring look, asking us to witness ourselves as embodied beings made in the idealised image of them. A great deal of this vision making takes place through the alchemy of spectacle where 'celebrities are the icons of media culture, the gods and goddesses of everyday life. To become a celebrity requires recognition as a star player in the field of media spectacle, be it sports, entertainment, or politics' (Kellner, 2003: 4). Celebrity spectacle is very much a fiction of enchantment.

The Enchantment of Celebrity Spectacle

The celebrity, who arrives in a limousine, at a red carpet event, is met with screams or ecstatic applause as they exit the car and are spotted by fanatical fans for the first time. The event will have been organised around a coordinated series of looking moments and visual encounters. The limousine is asked to stop at a particular vantage point, one that allows the celebrity to exit in full view of the commentators and news crews who are positioned within the cordon, armed with cameras. The celebrity exits the limousine in a ritualised moment that is meant to be captured and recorded, whether because of what they are wearing, or because of the way they deliver performative cues, such as a glittering smile or a graceful gait, which greets the armada of cameras and high-powered lenses set up before them.

The waiting fans are found in a tightly knit ring around the red carpet entrance, separated but connected to its splendour, its warm lights, its ornate glass doors, and they are asked to marvel at the proceedings as they unfold. They are positioned as star witnesses to the visual delights that are taking place all around them. These adoring fans will take photographs and videos of themselves at the event, of fellow fans, the glittering environment, and the celebrities as they arrive and leave. These treasured snaps and video footage will then be posted on Facebook or messaged to friends and family, evidence of them having being there and having taken part in the enchanted event. The celebrity event is a moment of pure, performative spectacle where, as Neal Gabler (2000) suggests, fans become artists acting out their role as leading characters on a show, or on stage, for their peers, who are cast as audience members. Their performance is there to be witnessed in a proceeding of grand intimacies.

The celebrity arrives at the event dressed to-be-looked-at, often in designer clothes that are themselves adverts to other visual texts, including this season's catwalk, and their next starring, upcoming role. They walk down the red carpet and pose at regular and regulated moments for photographers who are positioned to take iconic photographs. They will be interviewed, and their image will be relayed and replayed across any number of screens, newspapers, magazines, fanzines, and blogs right across the globe within seconds of their arrival, ready to be consumed no matter what the time of day or night.

The seeing of the celebrity crosses time and space thresholds producing an infinite number of widows and screens through which they can be viewed in. Seeing the celebrity is not an option but a condition of modern life. As Boorstin (1992) concludes, 'nothing is really real unless it happens on television'. Nothing is real unless a celebrity is witness to it or we witness a celebrity witnessing it. Nothing is real in the age of the spectacular:

> When the real world changes into simple images, simple images become real beings and effective motivations of a hypnotic behavior. The spectacle as a tendency to make one see the world by means of various specialized mediations (it can no longer be grasped directly), naturally finds vision to be the privileged human sense which the sense of touch was for other epochs. (Debord, 1977: section 18)

I would like to suggest that this privileging of vision manifests in five distinct but interrelated ways when it comes to seeing the celebrity. However, I would like to suggest that rather than their being an absent of touch in the visual world, as Boorstin suggested earlier, seeing often involves touching the celebrity with one's eyes.

The Celebrity Gaze

In contemporary life we are repeatedly invited to gaze longingly at the celebrity. The images that circulate of them are ones that often require a concentrated stare, a voyeuristic look, predominately built out of desire and longing. To appropriate Laura Mulvey's often quoted phrase, the celebrity is 'to-be-looked-at' (1975:9), positioned as an object of desire and as a subject of sexual enquiry and fascination. As celebrities, as exalted beings to a degree, the sexual attraction ignited by the gaze is heightened since they carry the markers of sexual perfection across a range of fiction and factual texts and contexts that they appear in.

In the cover shoot for the July 2012 edition of *Elle*, 'Selena Gomez: The New It Girl' is photographed in high-fashion outfits on a beach in Balmain. Gomez takes up the magazine's cover image and a three-page spread within it. She is described in the following way

> At only 19, Gomez is a mogul on the rise: a TV and music star, a fashion entrepreneur, and, as Justin Bieber's better half, the envy of Beliebers everywhere. Now, with a string of gritty indies on the horizon, she's poised to become Hollywood's newest It Girl.

Framed then as a renaissance star, the fashion shoot enacts the celebrity gaze to confirm her perfected nature. We are asked to stare longingly at her, posing in a metal chain Yves Saint Laurent dress that accentuate her curves, her breasts. Gomez faces the camera, the reader, and returns the stare, a smouldering look which has her red lips pursed. The bright sun and bleached sand provide a utopian space for desire to unfold. The shot involves both a chain of sexual connotations and fetish substitutions, including; her vulva-shaped red lips; the v-shaped chain dress (part masochistic and which draw our eyes to her breasts); and the ornate belt (with a buckle that represents, and which directs our eyes, to her vagina). This erotic mix occurs alongside her partly exposed flesh, all of which invite an eroticised stare, in a fantastic environment of sexual enchantment. We are asked to look longingly at Gomez, and beyond and through her dress, as if we (are like) lovers on a deserted beach.

The relay of the looks is obviously important here, as is the imagined gender of the gazer. Gomez stares back at what is positioned to be a young, female reader as if they are her love interest. While one can suggest a queering of the look here, it may well also be understood as a mirror where the female reader is being positioned to become the eyes and body of Gomez. The female reader is positioned to see herself in Gomez's gaze, and in an act of consuming is transformed into the very subject of a desiring and desirable being. Gomez embodies the look that the female reader wishes they could give, and in and through her, they can mirror this look and way of looking. They see themselves as Gomez on this secluded beach, occupying her erotic position, imagining that they are being looked at (by boys), returning their gaze, in a floating sea of enchanted meetings.

Elle encourages the reader to look, and to 'get her look, try Lancôme Color Design Pink Safari Palette for eyes, NARS lipstick in Jungle Red, and Lorac Tantalizer Highlighter and Matte Bronzer Duo'. The fashion shoot thus becomes a commodified makeover event. It suggests that through learning how to gaze intently, erotically, and by undertaking self-transformation through the right product purchases, one can become (like) Selena Gomez. One can argue that the gaze being learnt and embodied in this enchanted exchange is one purely built out of the heterosexual and patriarchal imagination. As Foucault argues, photography promotes 'the normalizing gaze, a surveillance that makes it possible to qualify, to classify and to punish. It establishes over individuals a visibility through which one differentiates and judges them' (1977: 25). In terms of celebrity culture, the gaze very often enacted positions women to see themselves as beautiful or not, based on physical ideals reproduced in the eyes of glamorous and famous women. If they see a mismatch then they may look to re-make themselves in the body of the celebrity they most admire or aspire to be like.

Contemporary cosmetic surgery and all manner of consumer products and beauty accessories are marketed as being able to create the look of the celebrity for the everyday person, a transformation made possible by a mirroring of *what they do I can become*, as this promotional flyer suggests

> Get the Facial Celebrities Swear By How do you suppose our best looking celebrities look so good? Maybe they regularly visit the award-winning Ilesha Haywood – The Paramedical Skin Clinic for the most effective skin treatments! (http://www.paramedicalskin-clinic.com.au/Meet-The-Expert.html)

This regeneration involves a doubling process, as Catherine Lutz and Jane Collins argue

> Mirror and camera are tools of self-reflection and surveillance. Each creates a double of the self, a second figure who can be examined more closely than the original – a double that can also be alienated from the self – taken away, as a photograph can be, to another place. (1994: 376)

However, this idea of doubling as the celebrity may not ultimately be self-alienating but life-determining and empowering. It can be argued that through this exchange one becomes a subject who controls the gaze rather than being an object of it. One (feels like) owns and controls the gaze, from a body position that recognises its carnal and affecting power. Sight thus becomes sense, and sensation becomes an affecting form of self-liberation. The girl who becomes Selena Gomez by internalising her look and through makeover changes, takes control of her eyes, and becomes aware of her body as performative and regenerative. If there is a queering of the look in this exchange, as I suggest above, then sexual identity itself registers as fluid, destabilising the binaries that hold together much of normative thinking.

While there is gender coding to the way we gaze at celebrities, I would suggest there is more democracy when it comes to who is fetishised and adored. The celebrity male pin-up, once centred on masculine postures and heterosexual iconography (Dyer, 1992), is now open to the same sexual signifiers as female celebrities (see the reading of the Crying Man series in Chapter 1). David Beckham's adverts for *Police* sunglasses contain the same set of erotic gaze signifiers as one does with the Selena Gomez fashion shoot; he is also to-be-looked-at, his perfected body is to be desired and consumed, by both men and women.

The celebrity gaze is also not singularly built on desire, or the desire to confirm the celebrity as an idealised being. The gaze can function as a way to investigate, explore the celebrity's authenticity, their truthfulness. The celebrity gaze can often be a critical one, either involving the search for proof that the celebrity is an authentic being, or for signs – stretch marks, a crooked smile, a false demeanour – that they are not what they say they are. However, when the gaze is involved in such deep levels of inspection it may be a different type of look that is being cast out.

The Celebrity Scan

The celebrity operates under a cultural microscope and is subject to forensic-like investigation by the media and the public. A range of digital technologies is used to reveal some aspect of a celebrity's life or behaviour to us. This revelation could be through the use of telescopic lenses by the paparazzi, or photo enhancement software deployed in gossip magazines to show something not visible to the naked eye. Very often what is being scanned is the exposure of celebrity skin or bare flesh, either as a focal point of eroticism, or to reveal the ugly, the blemished, the unclean; to capture celebrities 'off-guard, unkempt, unready, unsanitized' (Llewellyn-Smith, 2002: 120).

Gossip, celebrity-centred magazines often point to those areas in the photograph that reveal some hitherto hidden truth: they do the scanning and direct our gaze to the unsightly revelation that they have discovered on our behalf. The icon of a magnifying glass, and an arrow pointing to stretch marks, wrinkles, blotchy red eyes, or a fat belly, are the surveillance tools used by magazines to reveal THE TRUTH ABOUT...

Adam Knee (2006) suggests that so-called skin magazines, such as Celebrity Skin and Celebrity Sleuth, position the actor's bare body 'as a crucial site of authenticity, as that which reveals the truths hidden by publicist-controlled facial iconography and clothing' (163). Readers are left to scan what is presented to be an unaltered photograph, to discover the celebrity as they really are, stripped of fashionable clothes, and the artificial lights and flattering make-up supplied by the media industries. Filmed or photographed in dodgy hotel rooms, or else caught on low-resolution surveillance cameras, one gets to scan the deficiencies in their bodies. Although, as Knee recognises, very often these unaltered images are from authorised texts, and contribute to the myth of authenticity that the celebrity ultimately wants to be read through. Authenticity, even if it is unflattering, is of high currency value in celebrity culture.

Scanning can of course be put to diagnostic or 'medical' use, to confirm the body and/or face has had cosmetic surgery or implants, or is being wasted away by illness, drug use, and alcohol abuse. The often circulated 'before' and 'after' photographs of Michael Jackson's face position the reader to confirm the reshaping of his nose, the cheekbones, and eyes, and the whitening of his skin, as if this is a 'monstrous' makeover. In this form, the celebrity scan becomes a bio-political activity, a mechanism to exert control and power over the famous figure who is now reduced to a 'bare life' that we designate as either faulty or not.

Scanning involves the search for difference and Otherness, either to confirm one's superiority over the figure before us, or for identification purposes – I can now see that they are just like me. The before-and-after photographs of Michael Jackson can be read as confirming his flight from blackness as if he felt it to be inferior, was a mark on his skin. Or else it becomes a site (an insight) into the way race affected his self-image and self-esteem. It can ultimately be seen as positive, that Michael's flight from blackness drew attention to its/his beauty, before the anaemic beast of white culture took him over.

Such photographs draw one back, of course, to the celebrity metronome, to the swing that connects past and present together in a relentless beat of here/now and there/then. Michael Jackson's career is given its own private metronome, the tragic man behind the mask, the rise-then-fall trajectory, and a public metronome that measures, maintains, and crystallises attitudes to race, to ethnicity, to the idea of strangers and strangeness, across time and space.

The celebrity scan can be argued to increase the scepticism with which one views celebrities. The very devices that allow us to scan them have created a vision regime where we 'naturally' look for hidden things in the celebrity image; for the tell-tale signs of Photoshop technology; and for the use of air brushing software on them. We are suspicious of the celebrity image as much as we are seduced by it. However, this suspicion of the celebrity image can be argued to be part of a wider surveillance culture where doubt fuels paranoia, fuels the desire to survey, to scan, to report on all manner of things we see in the world as we go about our daily business. As a society we become encultured in the very apparatus that turn us into all-seeing beings.

Celebrity culture can be read as a culture of paranoid surveillance fuelled by the constant search for facts, omissions, falsehoods, and half-truths. Celebrity paranoia may very often be spectacular, when it becomes to a single event such as a courtroom drama, and it can be seen to ripple far and wide across the cultural landscape. For example, Mel Gibson's alleged tirade against Jews in July 2006, followed by the accusation that he made sexist and violent comments to his ex-partner, Oksana Grigorieva, in July 2010 – revealed through leaked police mug shots, recorded telephone conversations, and transcripts – is the spectacular substance out of which much of celebrity paranoia grows.

Trust is at issue here in what is perceived to be an age of 'faithless' activity and widespread corruption, where politicians are perceived to be as bent as the gangsters they covertly support. Celebrities ultimately become part of the age of conspiracy best exemplified through the way an 'accidental' celebrity death or suicide is read as murky and murderous. Marilyn Monroe and Kurt Cobain are two heightened examples of celebrity paranoia, where foul play has been suspected, fuelling a cultish search for evidence that proves the fact both were murdered.

But what if all I want to do is glimpse at a celebrity?

The Celebrity Glimpse

Celebrities are also glimpsed at, whereby something usually hidden from view (and often profane or taboo) is revealed for the briefest of moments. While this 'moment' will have often been photographed or videoed by the paparazzi or news crew, and then offered up to readers and viewers for repeated scanning, what intensifies the look is the sense that it is fleeting, impermanent, and that what we have witnessed is something transgressive at the exact moment it first took place.

The best, contemporary examples of the celebrity glimpse are those up-skirt shots that reveal a celebrity's genitals, as has happened with Britney Spears, Paris Hilton, and Lindsay Lohan as they exited limos; or those shots that expose a rogue nipple, as happened with Janet Jackson at the Super Bowl in 2004 (although this has since been scanned as deliberate, as performative act of self-promotion). The glimpse can also be of a celebrity who thinks the camera recording them has been turned off, only for a smirk or a darker mood to be revealed, as might be the case with the leaking of Mel Gibson's private telephone messages.

In terms of the on-the-fly, up-skirt shot, the glimpse reveals exactly what a female celebrity looks like in terms of her sex organs, and also how they groom themselves. This shot is of a different semiotic and experiential order than the scan because of its momentary qualities – the celebrity is out on the town, in movement, exiting or entering the limo to escape the media, or from the fans that surround their car. The paparazzi are jostling for position, in frenzied movement, hoping to get that one shot, the celebrity glimpse, that they can then sell to news providers. The celebrity glimpse has sizeable economic value not just for the photographer who snatches the shot but also for the newspaper that prints it because such revelatory pictures increase sales. And even though the shot disenchants the celebrity, the celebrity glimpse may increase their economic potential too.

While this celebrity glimpse is still taking place on a stage of sorts, and media rituals are in play, the certainty of the encounter being stage-managed is loosened because of the unpredictability of the event and its outcomes. The desire to get the shot itself, to glimpse the sex of the female celebrity, satisfies a desire to know the real person in the most private of places, and which cannot be read as 'inauthentic' in this context. Given these up-skirt celebrities are often represented as sexual and sexualised, the celebrity glimpse may confirm their status as ultimate sexual beings.

Through the celebrity glimpse, the female celebrity is being reduced to her biology, to pure sex, in the basest of ways. In this heterosexist, patriarchal glimpse, the knickerless celebrity with her perfectly waxed vulva, whom is too drunk to enter or exit her limo properly, loses her right to privacy as her private parts are revealed. The idea of personal grooming, however, returns us to the scan, and surveillance, since the glimpse invites a concentrated and invasive stare at the most intimate of places. As it does so, it continues and confirms a regime of self-reflective looking practices that all girls, women are meant to undertake. Finally, the glimpse of the celebrity's shaven vulva reveal something else: the contemporary trend of the juvenilisation of the female body, and the simultaneous fear of the unshaven vagina as something which might devour the glimpse as soon it is given.

The Celebrity Glance

The media and cultural context in which a celebrity is presented and represented produces different ways of looking at them. The glance or quick look, for example, has been attributed to television viewing, in contrast to the gaze, which has been seen as belonging to cinema. John Ellis suggests that the domestic context in which television viewing has historically taken place, with a host of likely distractions, in a context of constant programme flow and segmentation, produces a glance aesthetic in which the image isn't looked into deeply or for a sustained period of time (1982: 138). Television personalities, as Ellis calls them, employ direct address, or are tied to programmes where their, often ordinary, characters shine.

Television celebrity images are argued to have neither little of the replete photographic splendour nor the large size of the cinema screen, where film stars are born. There is less to-be–looked-at (of them) on television and so we glance at what is presented to us. One can take issue with this, of course, in a number of ways. Television is often cinematic and film stars take up television roles. Certain film and television genres involve lavish production design and an intensified continuity where there is a great deal to look or marvel at, and shifts in perspective that require focus. It is television that very often presents us with a spectacular media event, such as the Oscars. So, perhaps rather than there being *medium* differences, there are *media* differences that play both across film and television.

Quick looks and furtive glances are very much part of the fictive world of much of film and television. Characters repeatedly find themselves glancing at someone they admire or distrust or who they have a crush on. As viewers, we are meant to witness this glance; we are given privileged knowledge while everyone else in the diegetic world may remain unaware of it. That it is very often a celebrity playing to type, who throws this look, and who we are given special access to through this alignment in vision and knowledge, makes the glance a powerful identificatory tool in film and television. We are asked to see things they see while not being seen, a voyeuristic position of power that more generally circulates in celebrity culture.

Occasionally, however, there will be a relay of looks, as another character feels the glance and averts their gaze by looking up, down, or to the side (Dyer, 1982). In this context, the glance is felt as a scan or a gaze, and the character looks away. Very often it will be a male character glancing at a female character who will be forced to look away, both playing to celebrity type, an active male celebrity to passive female celebrity relational exchange. In this series of looks, between two gendered celebrities, power relations flow. The glance becomes an empowered look that produces a reactive gaze. The averted gaze, nonetheless, is very often positioned to be coy, to be receptive rather than reactionary. This game of looks is one played out in culture more generally where, as John Berger famously writes

> Men act and women appear. Men look at women. Women watch themselves being looked at ... The surveyor of woman in herself is male: the surveyed female. Thus she turns herself into an object – and most particularly an object of vision: a sight. (1972: 47)

In *Transformers* (Bay, 2007) Megan Fox is repeatedly the subject of voyeuristic looks and glances, both through an omnipotent camera that gazes at her curves, her midriff, her arms, legs, and breasts, and through attributed point of view shots by male characters, particularly Shia LaBeouf. In the 'car sequence', LaBeouf's car breaks down and Fox is filmed raising the bonnet and looking over the car's engine. A soft, warm, diffuse light bathes the scene and Fox is gazed at through a series of shots that focus on her body, fragmented into sexualised parts. The dialogue that accompanies the shots is full of innuendo, phallic references to 'double pumps' that 'can squirt the fuel so you can go faster', and 'nice headers', so the engine itself becomes a – or rather LaBeouf's – phallus. LeBeouf is captured glimpsing at Fox's midriff, her bottom, and is then given a point of view shot that gazes at Fox's body as he looks her up and down. The glimpse and the gaze combine and conjoin with the more general, omnipotent look of the camera, as Fox is sexualised and desired – a recurring motif of her star sign whether it is film roles, glamorous magazine spreads, or product endorsements. One can persuasively argue, to extend the understanding of the type of looking regime here, that LeBeouf employs his eyes (and the camera eye) to 'touch' Fox's body in this scene, engaging the viewer in a type of haptic sensory experience where what we see has embodied, tactile affects.

The Haptic Celebrity

Laura U. Marks (2000 has written that haptic visually is a more intimate form of looking, where 'the eyes themselves function like organs of touch' (162) and 'move over the surface of its object rather than plunge into illusionist depth, not to distinguish form so much as to discern texture' (ibid.). For Marks, film and video may be 'thought of as impressionable and conductive, like skin' (2000: xi–xii) and this sensory materiality is heightened by it containing

> [g]rainy, unclear images; sensuous imagery that evokes memory of the senses (i.e. water, nature); the depiction of characters in acute states of sensory activity (smelling, sniffing, tasting, etc.); close-to-the-body camera positions and panning across the surface of objects; changes in focus, under- and overexposure, decaying film and video imagery; optical printing; scratching on the emulsion; densely textured images, effects and formats such as Pixelvision ... and alternating between film/video. The haptic image is in a sense, 'less complete', requiring the viewer to contemplate the image as a material presence rather than an easily identifiable representational cog in a narrative wheel. (Totaro, 2002)

While Marks argues that haptic visuality is more common in experimental film and video, and situates it within the context of intercultural cinema, I think one can very readily apply it to the celebrity image wherever that image be sourced and found.

The celebrity image is very often sensuous and evokes the memory of sensation and erotic feeling. The still camera that captures them is often close to their body, the body that is often in a heightened state of arousal or of feeling deeply, and the moving camera tracks and pans, gazes and scans their bodies in close and proximate detail. Their skin and the conductive qualities of the screen that captures them seem to breathe through one another. The screens that celebrities are found in are often heavily textured, coloured with light and heat, and populated with objects and qualities that are themselves sensory driven (perfume bottles, tactile fabrics, ocean spray, beads of sweat, cigarette smoke, clouds drifting by). The celebrity emerges, then, through a haptic visuality where we touch them with the camera that records them, through our aligned eyes that are embodied apparatus. There is carnality, a celebaesthetic symbiosis, to the celebrity image and the way we touch them with our eyes.

In the Opium print advert, from Christmas 2000, actress Sophie Dahl is imaged naked, flat on her (arched) back, nestled in amongst some blue velvet never-ending sheets. Her legs are raised and wide apart, so that the shot resembles a frame from an erotic burlesque show, or porn film, or a Glamour Shoot. Dahl has her right hand upon one breast, her red mouth open and pursed, her head raised from the floor and tilted back, with her vibrant red hair tossed back, and falling away into the darkness that surrounds her. Our eyes are being employed to not only see but to move across and touch her body, and the sensory materials and trinkets that near envelope her. Her ultra white skin lights up the image but rather than the 'whiteness' being translucent and ethereal, there is texture to the white skin, as if it is made of chalk, alabaster, or ice. The gold, glittering high-heel shoes and the gold choker chain around her neck enact the perfect fetish. She writhes – I imagine *movement* in this still image – in the grip, the peak/plateau of the ultimate orgasm. She moans – I imagine *sound* emanating from this still image – in the throes of this quivering body. I see, hear, and touch the body and walk around the room that it is found in.

The mise-en-scene suggests that this white starlet is addicted to sex and the pleasures of the sexual climax, so much so that it is actually killing her. Although the 'heroin-chic' of the Opium advert could also be read as a type of celebrity death, the whiter-than-white skin being the result of a draining away of life as the 'drug' (fame) repeatedly pumps through her expectant veins. Of course, there are also clear sexual/phallic connotations to this idea of blood pumping into/through/away from the white celebrity body. The Yves Saint Laurent Opium lettering on the side of the advert almost enters her open legs, confirming a scene of penetration.

This whiter-than-white celebrity female body is also, then, *all death*, a corpse-like figure, one that has just perhaps exhaled her last icy breath. I also imagine *stillness* and silence in this billboard and magazine advert. The illicit drug (the extravagances of a celebrity life?) that has given her so much pleasure/freedom is also the drug that has taken her life. Dahl has entered into a willing, masochistic relationship with her celebrity body until the fix that is needed for plenitude, is also the fix that kills her. The celebrity body in this advert is simultaneously erotic and eroticised, made of living, masturbatory flesh, and horrid and horrifying, a sex-death corpse, emptied of life. Dahl, of course, or so it has been reported, went from a size 16 to a size 8, literally emptying herself of corporeal fullness.

In the Opium advert we witness – as if we are there – this life-and-death wrestle over the female celebrity's body. We witness a struggle between the desires which bring life and death to the celebrity: between the best ever fuck that removes Sophie Dahl from the binds of patriarchal repression, and one that brings her closer to, into the arms of, death itself, perhaps as a punishment for, or a release from, the extremes of her celebrity life.

Chris Rojek has suggested that for the celebrity the split between the 'I' (the private or veridical self) and the 'me' (the self presented to the world) is 'often disturbing. So much so, that celebrities frequently complain of identity confusion and the colonization of the veridical self by the public face' (2001:11). The celebrity can lose their own sense of authentic self in the artifice of the celebrity 'I' as the trappings of fame, and its relentless spotlight, allow no private time to emerge.

In response, Rojek suggests, celebrities can behave badly as a way of revealing the anguish they face as divided identities. The train wreck celebrity, the celebrity compulsive, and the promiscuous celebrity can be understood as attempts to annihilate one half of the divided self. In this respect, the Britney Spears 'head shaving' incident in 2009 may well be an example of her trying to eradicate the blonde, feminine persona that defined her as a certain type of sexualised celebrity (Redmond, 2011). In the Opium advert, similarly, what may be being played out is the struggle between the I and the Me of celebrity culture as it manifests in the tactile body of Sophie Dahl. Further, in terms of the reader's positioning, the Opium advert may be eliciting the very desire to love and kill our celebrities with our eyes that are acting as desiring, murderous organs of touch. Such a haptic relationship is so much further intensified when our look emerges in the form of a close-up.

The Celebrity Close-Up

The media to suggest that a report, interview, or feature will be intimate and revelatory often uses the phrase, 'the celebrity in close-up'. The close-up is a metaphor in this context for unmediated access, as if the private self behind the celebrity mask is to be revealed. We are asked to read, listen, or watch because we will learn new things about the celebrity. For example, heartfelt and confessional information may be shared that will confirm, extend, or change our perception of them. A Z100 trending article in June 2012, for example, suggests

> Rihanna is set to reveal all about her life, loves and recent health woes in a candid TV special with Oprah. The TV talk show queen has landed an in-depth interview with RiRi and insiders insist nothing will be off-limits.

In April 2011, Demi Lovato revealed in an 'exclusive' interview with *People* magazine that she was bipolar and that she 'battled depression from a very young age'. Such a revelation is used by her (and the magazine) to explain her violent mood swings, which were very often in the public eye. Lovato is lauded for doing so and is subsequently used in health awareness raising sites such as Goodtherapy.org as a model for young people also suffering from bipolar disease.

However, it seems to be a condition located with celebrities in general; that they are innately or essentially closer to mental illness in all its forms, be it malady, melancholy, bulimia, anorexia nervosa, various alcohol, drug and sex addictions, or hysteria and depression (Harper, 2006). When it comes to female celebrities, particularly those defined as toxic, the types of mental illness they suffer and the presentations and representations of them are often differently encoded. The 'mentally ill' female celebrity is often placed in legalistic and judicial care, framed as needing patriarchal law to protect, control, and make them well again. The apparatus of the telephoto lens will often be used to capture them in a state of some distress, a shot that evidences and justifies their designation as mentally ill.

The close-up as a photographic and cinematic technique, however, reveals the 'truth' of the celebrity through the power of total sight. The close-up shot doesn't need words, textual anchorage, soundtrack, or context necessarily, for this truth to be revealed. The power of the close-up is one that is suggested to reveal all, physically, emotionally, existentially, as it leaks personal history and trauma. We are asked to look into the image and see the celebrity as they really are. The close-up of the face may capture the celebrity in a state of pure perfection, as if they descended from the heavens. Their physical and emotional beauty will be there on their skin and the skin of the image, for all to see. As Barthes writes of the close-up in relation to Greta Garbo

> Offered to one's gaze a sort of Platonic Idea of the human creature ... The name given to her, the Divine, probably aimed to convey less a superlative state of beauty than the essence of her corporeal person, descended from a heaven where all things are formed and perfected in the clearest light. (Barthes, 2007: 261)

One can argue that the close-up allows the viewer or reader to 'touch' and feel a gesture, a look: to see the fine lines of a cheek, since the face of a celebrity stays close to them in an intensified field of vision. In the close-up, there is only 'you' and the celebrity in a one-to-one relational exchange. The space in and between you and the celebrity is evaporated, creating a proximity or closeness of utmost intimacy. Strong identifications emerge through the affecting power of the close-up. Of course, not all close-ups are of the celebrity's face – it might be of a connected object, costume, or, in the 'up-skirt' context mentioned above, of celebrity flesh or sex. In these contexts, objects are faceified, fabrics and colours sensationalised, and body parts sexualised, with little distance between viewer or reader and the celebrity. For Deleuze, faciality involves the combination of a

> reflecting, immobile unity and of intensive expressive moments which constitutes the affect ... Each time we discover these two poles in something we can say that this thing has been treated as a face (visage): it has been 'envisaged' or faceified (visage-fiee) and in turn stares at us. (1986: 87–88)

This idea that close-ups of possessions, objects, and body parts involves a returning of the gaze, channelling affect and an intensive response from the reader or viewer, has particular resonance with regards to celebrity culture. In close-up, they become auratic objects, fetishised fabrics, touched or worn by the celebrity, with their personal imprint on them, staring back at us in co-synaesthesia union and communion. Or, if they are close-ups of parts of the celebrity body these dissections become super-iconic blocks of sensation that register as reactive gazes.

The cultural or entertainment context that the close-up is situated in is also important: in a gossip magazine we may be being positioned to scan the celebrity image for signs of hurt following a relationship bust up; in a movie magazine we may be being asked to gaze at the image and the beauty of the film star captured at their perfected best; and in a confessional context, we may be being positioned to glimpse at the close-up, to see the 'taboo' in whatever form it is being framed in. The close-up itself can be experienced in different ways across the career of a celebrity, or it can be read in contradictory ways at any one moment in time. Today's celebrity close-up may reveal joy and happiness, while tomorrow's close-up may reveal pain and anguish, and yet the order of these 'captured moments' can be reversed to reveal a different temporal logic to a celebrity's well-being. We revisit close-ups long after the event, with a new timeline of their life in place, and see and feel something different from the first time we gazed upon it. This is particularly true when a revelation forces us to see an 'old' close-up in a new light – something that has recently happened with the Jimmy Savile paedophile scandal where we re-revisit past images to find the perversity in them.

The celebrity close-up has its own metronome, and it is ticking softly, then loudly, then perhaps softly again across time and space. One film star whose signification and sensorial streams rises and falls in the way they are captured in 'close-up' is Tom Cruise.

Cruise in Close-Up

One of Cruise's key star and performative signifiers and affective registers (like so many film stars) is the close-up centred on his smiling face. Cruise in close-up is above else a beaming smile designated as warm and romantic. Nonetheless, one also finds his face caught by the paparazzi in an 'unauthorised' moment on the street, at a red carpet event, or in other public contexts, where he is being photographed and pursued. In this context, Cruise's face has been captured to tell a lie, or to reveal an inner truth he is unconsciously confessing, which he may be uncomfortable with revealing. There are also performative and self-reflexive cues to the close-up of Cruise's face, which relate to the alleged ambiguity over his sexuality and to the criticisms that he is all auratic artifice and no performative depth. In these shifting contexts, one can argue that the close-up on Tom Cruise's face works in one of four contradictory ways.

Close-up as confirmation

First, the close-up of Cruise's face confirms and re-affirms his heterosexual, romantic star-self, whether this be in the diegetic context of the film he may be appearing in, or in the promotional and marketing shots and magazine shoots that circulate more widely in media culture. Cruise's smiling or desiring face has appeared on the covers of numerous magazines, across their US and international editions, including *Vanity Fair* (October 1994), *Rolling Stone* magazine (June 1986), *Premiere* (July 1988), *Time* magazine (June 2002), *People* magazine (July 1996, December 2008), and *GQ* (May 2006, December 2011). Each of these covers captures Cruise smiling, emoting desire and desirability. The heavenly close-ups are contextualised in terms of an upcoming film release; or personal matters that the magazine might have an 'exclusive' on; or on trying to examine the 'real' Cruise beneath the star image. In each case, the close-up is meant to capture his handsomeness, honesty, and integrity. In these confirming contexts, Cruise is very often a beautiful face that reveals an essential beauty within him.

In all of Cruise's films there will be a series of signalled moments where the camera will cut to his face to capture the smile, or an eroticised stare or gaze. The smile or desiring stare not only relates to his attraction to a female character in the film, but the implied viewer who sees it beaming just for them. In *Top Gun* (Scott, 1986), where Cruise plays Maverick, an ace fighter pilot, he is continually captured in close-up shots, wearing aviator sunglasses, while smiling or returning a desiring look back at the camera; back at his love interest Charlie (played by Kelly McGillis); and at the viewers in the auditorium.

Nonetheless, the romantic close-up can be read critically since his face is not one that captures 'the fine grain of restrained mannerisms' (King, 2008: 125) but mere physical perfection. Cruise's face is all 'body' and no brain, a flaccid substitute for his beef-cake persona. Or it is a narcissistic mirror that reveals only the surface-level appeal of Cruise's stardom and not the depth of a serious actor.

Close-up crisis

Second, the close-up of Cruise's face is employed to question, undermine, or trouble what is imagined or alleged to be his 'constructed' perfected heterosexuality. Under the close-up, in this context, one is asked to see in the Cruise face a feminine, or queer self, normally hidden from the public eye. Cruise thus becomes a troubled heterosexual star who is simultaneously masculine and feminine: androgynous, and also, potentially, queer.

This counter-reading can emerge through the way close-ups are read in the context of a Cruise film, across his oeuvre, or through fanzines, blogs, and discussion boards that read his face against the grain of normative heterosexuality. Cruise's face, then, is very often the subject/object of the queer gaze inviting desire from gay men, who see Cruise returning this desire through its 'open' concealment. Cruise's character in *Top Gun*, Maverick, has been read in this way, with the close-up seen as a way of positioning him as outside of heteronormative relations, returning a queer look.

Close-up authenticity

Third, and in direct contradiction to the observation made above, the close-up of Cruise's face is employed to authenticate his performative or actorly self. Through the close-up one can see that Cruise's face *can* emote, that it can respond to dramatic action with an affecting intensity that counts as gifted acting. One is meant to discern realism – a phenomenological truth – in the actorly Cruise close-up. In *Magnolia*, for example, there is a 20-second close-up on Cruise's face, playing the part of misogynist and cult therapist, Frank T. J. Mackey. The shot of Cruise's face is set against a darkened, enveloping background. It is only his face, still but perplexed, that we are directed to focus upon. We are asked to gaze at the face and to scan it. In this scene, he is asked by the off-screen interviewer what he is doing and he responds, after an extended pause, with 'I am quietly judging you'. The self-reflexive relay between the two characters here is disturbing, conjoined as it is with this close-up of Cruise's wounded face. Cruise looks into us as we look into him in what becomes a challenging visual relay. In one sense, it becomes a meta-commentary on the way Cruise-the-star is being constantly judged by the media. In an other sense, it draws attention to Cruise's own complex psyche, and to the complexity of the character he is playing.

Close-up parody

Finally, the close-up of Cruise's face is self-reflexively employed to reveal his star artifice and to render the Cruise brand as 'hysterical'. In this context, we are meant to recognise the Cruise signifiers as cliché, and we are asked to lampoon him, as was most notably the case in the scientology spoof scene in *Superhero Movie* (Mazin, 2008). Cruise's persona is imagined to be so over-determining that we can only be ever watching Cruise play Cruise:

> Cruise is entertaining in this role and others, and he does nothing that adversely effects 'Collateral', outside the fact that his mere presence is distracting, and he is not quite adept at transformation. He is Tom Cruise, with grey hair, carrying a gun. (Little, 2004)

All four types of the Cruise close-up circulate in media culture today. Which one might be foregrounded at any one time depends on the film roles chosen, the film's success, the interviews undertaken, and the type of gossip and innuendo being communicated. The media context is also important, and so is whether the close-up shot is authorised, snapped, or doctored and manipulated. Cruise's own star image exists as a series of metronome swings with each beat a sound of contestation.

In the digital age, of course, it is near impossible to control the flow of images or how they might be reconstituted. We have been given extraordinary eyes with which to see things in the modern world. His own metronome draws together past and present, and its ticking softens or loudens, slows or quickens, depending on his newsworthiness, marketability, and the frenzy or paucity of images that surround him. Cruise is in close-up one day, a long shot the next; his voice dominates news coverage this month, and is barely a whisper the next. His star image rises and falls, its threads prominent and vibrant this season but ochre and marginal the next. Cruise exists as a complex media representation that requires some investigation.

Star Images: Tom Cruise

Tom Cruise is a media representation; his star image comes into existence through the circulation of related and relatable behaviours, values and actions, communicated in film roles, advertorial and marketing work, interviews and commentaries. Cruise is situated within narrative, fictive, and factual frameworks that draw on his star image to propel fantasises, desires, and to enact heroic individualism and the promise of heterosexual romantic coupling. These frameworks also often question his legitimacy as a star and actor. These representations are part of wider discourses where issues to do with identity and difference are played out, where 'Images do not simply reflect, but organizes and constructs our sense of reality' (Storey, 2001: 59). Cruise functions as an idealised white male, masculine and authentic. However, he can also be deconstructed as a star whose sign system collapses binaries and opens up a space for queer and transgressive impulses to emerge. Finally, in the contemporary sense, there has emerged a parodic Cruise, who lampoons his own star image. There seems, then, to be three different and competing Cruise star images in circulation.

Ideal Tom Cruise

The films that Cruise stars in (and which he often produces) revolve around a set of articulating narrative structures and behavioural qualities. At the level of the film text, Cruise signifies as an ideal and idealised heroic, heterosexual, all-American white male. In his starring roles he is often an action hero, with a hard, skilful, bronzed body that succeeds in its missions after overcoming trials and tribulations. Cruise will often be blue collar, a maverick, or outsider in some way, and yet the ideology that surrounds his roles endows him with the state of American exceptionalism. Cruise embodies the myth of the hero and epitomises the steps taken by the hero's journey to overcome what may stand in their way. As I have argued elsewhere, in *War of the Worlds* (Spielberg, 2005), Tom Cruise (Ray Farrier) is a

> [b]lue-collar worker from New Jersey, estranged from his family, who during the course of the film proves his worth as a Father/heroic male. Not quite the mythic fire fighter of 9/11, Ferrier nonetheless crawls through the rubble, the twisted metal, and the burning fires to keep his children/child alive ... His heroic actions refuse to let

America be over-taken, over-run, and he will protect America from wayward Americans. Ferris (Cruise) stands, then, as a symbol of America's resilience and hyper-masculine strength when it is tested most. (Redmond, 2008:12).

In his films, Cruise is also a campaigner, a seeker of justice, and is ethically driven by the founding principles of the American Constitution and neo-liberal individualism. In films such as *Born on the 4th of July* (Stone, 1989), *A Few Good Men* (Reiner, 1992), *Jerry Maguire* (Crowe, 1996), and *Valkerie* (Singer, 2008), Cruise wants to end an injustice, right a cultural wrong, or bring an evil person to justice. He exists on the side of law and order as it is ideally imagined.

Cruise is of course very often a romantic lead, with a killer smile, a beautiful body and face, and his love interest will confirm his desirability and normative, reproductive heterosexuality. Cruise is regularly and readily fallen in love with by his beautiful, female co-stars. At the end of *Jerry Maguire* not only has his character become ethical in the job he does, but he also gets the girl of his dreams. In a dramatic scene at their house, in front of Dorothy's (played by Renée Zellweger) friends, Jerry (Cruise) tells her that she completes him, tears rolling down his cheeks as he does so. The romantic embrace and kiss cements the utopian sentiments. That Dorothy famously responds with, 'you had me at hello', positions Cruise as the ultimate male lead. All these ideal and idealised constituents combine to produce a coherent Cruise star image that mirrors and reproduces the dominant ideology of contemporary America.

The coherency of Cruise's star image is authenticated by facts circulated about him and through authorised interviews and confessions. We know through various media accounts that he is an extreme sports enthusiast, including pro-level rock climber, racing driver, and parachute jumper; and that, consequently, he does most of his own stunts, authenticating his action hero status. We also know that Cruise has employed the Method style of acting, for example, through spending six weeks as a Fed Ex deliverer, and through gun use and action training to learn the skills and behavioural characteristic of his assassin character in *Collateral* (Mann, 2004). We know through various reports that Cruise has dyslexia; was bullied as a kid; and allegedly suffered child abuse. He has been married three times and has only found true love with Katie Holmes, an idealised female star. His confessional outpouring of his love for Katie on the *Oprah Winfrey Show*, with her waiting in the wings, was meant to reveal the real Tom Cruise. He has a family, with adopted and natural children that he adores.

Cruise then embodies the myth of the American dream, the success myth, that anyone can make it if they are talented and work hard enough at their goals. Through Cruise it is prophesised that American capitalism will reward the hard worker, no matter what their background or disadvantage. As a family man he cherishes and lives out America's core values. Cruise is ultimately a type of ideological social glue that binds the values, beliefs, and activities of American society together in one fantastic, mythic space. But it may be a queer space, also.

Queer Cruise

The controversy that surrounds Cruise's authenticity, religious leanings, and sexuality has left his star image vulnerable: he is repeatedly framed as more freak than icon. Cruise is ageing, he turned 50 in July 2012, and he is a devoted family man who cannot keep his family together. A disjuncture thus emerges between youthful heterosexual idealisation and the waning facts of his lived, living body; the controversies that surround his life; and his happily-ever-after married status that keeps disintegrating. The I and Me of his star sign begin to dislocate, fracture, and as such the coherency of his representations loosens and contest one another.

In terms of Cruise's sexuality, at the level of the film text, there is (and perhaps always has been) something about the way that he embodies masculinity that doesn't quite cohere or ring true. What emerges is a space of sexual instability in which 'already queerly positioned viewers can connect with in various ways, and within which straights can express their queer impulses' (Doty, 1993: 21) One can argue that through this gender and sexual ambivalence, Cruise cracks open the ideological work of patriarchy.

First, to return to the employment of the close-up, Cruise's feminine, or boyish face, invites a queer gaze. Second, his masculine roles and buddy relationships can be read as moving from the homosocial to ones built on male desire and shared longings. In nearly all of Cruise's films there are dominant and dominating male relationships that he is involved in and they very often overpower the role of the female character who can be argued to exist to simply 'straighten' the sexual impulses in his work. One can productively offer a queer reading of *Top Gun*, for example, in terms of male bonding, body display, double entendre dialogue exchanges, and the sharing of intimate spaces. The shower scene, in which Cruise (Maverick) is challenged by Kilmer (Iceman) with the lines 'whose side are you on' can be read as a call to recognise his queer self and to reject heterosexuality. Both are naked apart from towels that cover their genitals, their bodies are toned, muscular and wet, and they are both positioned in desiring poses. At the end of *The Last Samurai* (Zwick, 2003), Cruise (playing Nathan Algren) intimately embraces the dying Samurai Warrior Katsumoto (played by Ken Watanabe), as cherry blossoms fall from the trees. This can be read as a romantic coupling of two men deeply in love with one another.

Finally, the characters that Cruise plays very often seem to be unable to love, to be intimate with, or to make love, to other women in his films. Very often Cruise is denied the chance to consummate his desires that are thwarted or misplaced, or else they are perverted in some way. In *Jerry Maguire* and *Vanilla Sky* (Crowe, 2001) he makes love to women who turn him off, or repulse him, and we see that etched onto his recoiling face. In *Eyes Wide Shut* (Kubrick, 1999) his relationship to Kidman is sterile, mechanical, and he goes on a quest or search to find his true sexual self. In his films, relationships break down, women are killed, and Cruise's appearance suggests an existential crisis of sorts. Very often there is a 'gap' between film character and star image through which a traumatised Cruise emerges. His slow death, alone on a nowhere train at the end of *Collateral*, is a powerful signifier of the Cruise persona falling back down to earth and expiring.

Cruise has fallen back down to earth because of the facts circulated in the media that counter his idealised image. In this context, he is an inauthentic, plastic star whose public and private self draws attention to the machinery of the star system. He is a high-profile advocate for the Church of Scientology, which is reported to be a pseudo religion with dedicated followers. His leaked promotional video for the church, in which he counsels, 'I know I can help' when describing what he might do at the scene of a crash, evidence of messianic grandeur. Cruise is reported to be a 'control freak' in all aspects of his life. In this context, Katie is seen as a 'prisoner in a loveless marriage' (*US Weekly*, July 2012 or she has to follow Cruise's wishes and commands, including remaining silent during the labour and birth of their daughter (*MSNBC Today*, 2005). Cruise's notable public criticisms of psychiatry and the use of anti-depressive drugs have attracted controversy and media interest, positioning him as ill-informed and as patriarchal and misogynist. At this time (the 2006–2008 period) Cruise's box office ratings fell, notably with *Mission Impossible 3* (Abrams, 2006), and his 14-year relationship with Paramount Pictures came to an end because of his 'erratic behaviour' (*CNN Money*, August, 2006). In 2012 Katie Holmes filed for divorce and rumours circulated of Cruise having auditioned various women for the role of wife that Holmes eventually won. Such a recasting of their relationship returns us to the confessional moment on *Oprah*, re-signing it as a performance of grand gestures and fake intimacy. How has Cruise and his cultural intermediaries responded to the crisis in the Cruise star image?

Parodic Cruise

Cruise's star image now increasingly involves parodic excess and the explicit undermining of his masculine self. In films such as *Tropic Thunder* (Stiller, 2008), *Knight and Day* (Mangold, 2010), and *Rock of Ages* (Shankman, 2012), he either plays against type, or the film self-reflects on his star image. In *Tropic Thunder*, Cruise is bald, fat, and wears spectacles, playing the role of foul-mouthed movie producer, Les Grossman. As the credits roll at the end of the film, he is filmed dancing, gyrating, mocking his own idealisation and the movie industry that produced him. In *Knight and Day*, the film plays on a series of allusions to his star image, as his assassin skills are mocked and recast as playful and ironic. We are not being asked to take this version of Cruise seriously. In *Rock of Ages*, Cruise plays long-haired, has been Stacee Jaxx, former lead singer of Arsenal, the biggest rock band in the world, who has fled to Latin America to evade certain crimes that he committed in the United States. *Rock of Ages* is a comedy-musical, re-situating the Cruise star image into new genres that will rely less on his idealised, masculine self.

The Cruise star image is undergoing a process of transformation and renewal. Cruise of course has just starred in the very successful *Mission Impossible 4* (Bird, 2011), and so he also remains the Cruise we have known through numerous action film iterations. Cruise's star tapestry now involves new threads, then, as he further splits and extends into various representational signs; and because the new social media and digital interfaces readily provide contestations over and over again. The Cruise metronome of course has a different rhythm as he gets older, as more of his images, stories, facts, omissions, allegations, revelations, and confessions circulate and collide. Cruise's past, present, and future star-self sound out, and in this culture of sight, are there for everyone to see (and hear).

Tom Cruise (stone, silence, oil, syrup, surface, cold).

3 Buying Celebrity

I am holding my partner's hand as Lana Del Rey arrives on stage wearing a red dress and high heels. I lean in, kiss my partner's neck, as the sounds of Del Rey's doom-laden torch songs rise up. Video images of Americano are projected behind her, and the stage is filled with plastic greenery. Del Rey slowly moves, pouts perfectly, as she takes her high heels off, honey. The crowd scream; I hold my partner tightly. Del Rey's album has been the soundtrack to our blossoming love, and being here together will help cement our relationship further. We have been sold on Del Rey's version of romance.

Bieber Fever

The celebrity exists in an orgy of promotions, and celebrity culture can be argued to sustain itself through a series of synergetic, commercial industries, practices and processes that produce commodities for consumption purposes. In this guise, the celebrity exists as a key engine in late or liquid capitalism's pursuit of individualised living through the politics of buying and selling objects endowed with higher-order meaning. Liquid capitalism suggests that life is made meaningful in and through glamorous lifestyle choices best embodied by celebrities. That these celebrity commodities are disposable, have a limited life span, and can and should be replaced, creates a culture of constant consumption exchange where fads and fashion trends produce a never-ending stream of new idols and new commodities to identify with and purchase.

The celebrity is a brand; their performances (on or off stage, public or private) are marketing and self-promotion exercises. The celebrity sells products and services through public events, endorsements, and lifestyle choices; and they encourage the practices of consumption through being idealised commodity vessels. It is through the way they live their day-to-day lives that the values of consuming and consumption are perfectly realised. We often see celebrities shopping, dining out, dressed in designer clothes and accessories, or we see them fly off overseas to some exotic holiday destination. Celebrities are dream factories and they manufacture longings, desires, aspirations, and ambitions as a string of pretty things that should be possessed if one is to be happy, satisfied, and useful – since to consume is classified as the activity that ultimately makes one a good and productive citizen (Weber, 2009). Contemporary celebrity culture is at the heart of the neo-liberal project where '[m]arket forces have begun to model institutional life and press deeply into our private lives, as well as dominating political discourse. They have shaped a popular culture that extols celebrity and success and promotes values of private gain and possessive individualism' (Hall, 2013).

One can make critical sense of celebrity culture as comprised of a series of 'commercial intertexts' where a range of products and services are being displayed and marketed at any one time, every time a celebrity is seen in public, or is connected to a media genre they may be performing in, or is seen appearing in an advert or promotions of some sort. Liquid capitalism turns the celebrity into a product line and the audience into consumers.

In July 2012 Justin Bieber appeared on Channel 7's *Australia's Got Talent* and performed two songs, *As Long as You Love Me* (introduced as his new single, 'out now') and *If I Was Your Boyfriend*, the second 'global smash hit' from his best-selling album *Believe* (2012). The Got Talent format is now an international franchise, first developed in the UK and owned by Simon Cowell's SYCOtv Company. There are 39 countries that have a version of the show in which aspiring entertainers battle it out to be crowned the country's most talented individual.

Bieber's appearance on *Australia's Got Talent*, designated a grand final, markets his own star-celebrity image; promotes his new single and album; his back catalogue; his forthcoming tour of Australia (announced in the 'interview' segment of the show); the branded clothes he is wearing; the channel the show appears on; its media partners and subsidiary companies; and the show itself and its 'authentic' commitment to finding new, raw talent. This is something that Bieber directly validates since his own narrative of success is built upon being 'found' after posting several notable home-made singing performances on YouTube.

Bieber produces the cult and commodified culture of celebrity. He appears on stage to wild screams, pulsating lights, frenetic camera work, a sea of placards and banners that spell out his name, and the hysteria he produces in his girl fans (labelled 'Bieber fevers'). He appears on stage through two doors, which he pushes back, with smoke and lights signalling his auratic arrival. Bieber sings of romantic love, heartache, and desire, to electronic pop beats with catchy choruses that can be relayed, chanted back. Dancing girls and boys appear on his either side and they step and move in easy, quick-time formation. This is their chance to be noticed, to also be in the spotlight.

Every time Bieber moves a little closer to the audience he is greeted with loud screams, captured by a mobile camera that repeatedly cuts to the faces of young girls on the teary verge of ecstasy. They desire him absolutely as they imagine that he sings to and for each of them, or that his lyrics are confessional and intimate, or that he is as 'love-struck' as they are. Widely reported in the media, Bieber's romantic love affair with the equally beautiful Selena Gomez, imaged through glamorous shots of them holding hands, roots affection to the lifestyle choices they embody and which re-emerge in the 'body' of the lyrics he sings. He sings for Gomez. He sings for girls who see themselves as Gomez – the idealised and sexualised Gomez on the utopian beach, wearing that Yves Saint Laurent dress (see Chapter 2 for a discussion of this image).

These teenage girls search for authenticity, for true moments of shared and reciprocated intimacy with Bieber, but this is a search connected to purchasing his records, going to his shows, or through buying those magazines and ancillary products that he appears in or is connected to. The fever he is connected to is commodified heterosexual romanticism. The fever he creates is intimately tied to buying and owning Bieber merchandising, product endorsements, collectables, posters, sneakers, and *the scent of Bieber*. This, then, is the intimacy of consumption as it is manufactured and circulated. Each of his items of clothing is branded goods, as is his trademark hairstyle. Bieber's skin is flawless, acne free, the result of using Pro-active acne cream, a product he endorses. From head-to-toe Bieber is a production line and the viewer a consumer of his goods. As Ellis Cashmore contends

All celebrities exhibit themselves in a way that makes them resemble merchandise — articles of trade that can be bought and sold in the marketplace. Like Beyoncé, they help sell products, from movie tickets, DVDs, and cds to the cars, colognes and the designer labels they customarily endorse. They also embody exchange values. As such, they are living commodities themselves: their very presence, whether at a première or at the gym, has value, if for no other reason than we are interested enough to pay for it (how many celebrity magazines feature pictures of stars driving, shopping or just doing nothing in particular? (2010: 147)

Bieber sells the ideology of the show which is made in the image of celebrity culture: that if you have talent you can make it (as he did) and that if you make it you will have success, adulation, fame, and fortune, which will be enacted through a replete consumption lifestyle. Bieber is imagined to have *achieved* celebrity status and this is something the show seeks to also produce the myth of – only the most talented will win through.

During the interview segment we are told numerous facts that confirm Bieber's star-celebrity status, including the facts that his album is number 1 in 30 countries; his videos have a combined 3 billion YouTube hits; he has over 44 million followers on Facebook; and that the night before the live performance on the show, his Twitter following had grown to over 25 million. The interviewer frames Bieber as one of the most successful and deserving of contemporary pop stars because he 'wrote most of his latest album', but this endorsement is a projection of the show's own desire to see it validated through his appearance on it. What is also in promotional circulation is the social media, to which the show is also connected through its Facebook page. In short, a dynamic set of product placement exchanges is seamlessly taking place across a number of media sites and industries through Bieber's star turn.

Girls continue to scream; one rushes the stage and is then pulled away by one of the judges (Brian McFadden). This leads to newspaper headlines (and the hope of increased sales with it), and a further set of promotional devices that propel Bieber and the show into national and international cultural visibility. The fracas also connects to McFadden's own rebel-rouser star status. The channel's own website posts footage of the performance, and Bieber's public relations team are on hand to ensure that his appearance gets widely reported in international contexts, through other media outlets.

Bieber constantly tweets how much he loves Australia and his Facebook page is scattered with photos of his time there. A Bieber collector's edition of the monthly teenage girl's magazine, *Girlfriend*, is published the week that Bieber is in Australia, full of pictures of Bieber, relevant 'star' facts, a rags-to-riches biography, and confessional details about his inner feelings. These are meant to then become cherished mementoes of, and access points to, his time in Australia for Bieber's legions of fans.

Channel 7 is owned by Seven West Media, which also own The West Australian, the leading metropolitan newspaper in Western Australia; 21 West Australian regional newspapers; nine regional radio stations; Pacific Magazines which publish amongst others, *Girlfriend*; the weekly celebrity magazine, *Famous*; and the monthly television guide, *TV*

Hits. Seven West Media also have 50 per cent interest in Yahoo! 7, one of Australia and New Zealand's leading online media platforms, and a 33 per cent share in Sky News Australia. All of these outlets published stories of, or reported on, Bieber the week he appeared on *Australia's Got Talent*. Yahoo! 7 offered viewers a sneak preview of his performance, with *Girlfriend* publishing as the Bieber collector's edition (see above). Channel 7 has established output deals with a number of American production studios, including NBC Universal, The Walt Disney Company, and ABC Studios. NBC Universal has a relationship with The Island Def Jam Music Group, who has a share in the record label that Bieber is signed to.

The branding of Bieber, then, involves a complex series of cross-media promotions and alliances that takes one from clothes, hair, and acne cream, to the synergetic operations of multimedia corporations selling records, tours, television shows, newspapers, and the social media. Celebrity branding takes place in what Maureen Orth (2003) defines as the 'celebrity-industry complex', where images, products, goods and services from a vast range of companies, often intimately connected, are mass-produced for mass consumption.

If one was to take a Disney star such as Hilary Duff or Miley Cyrus one can discern how their image is circulated and sold through all the different companies connected to this transnational corporation: television, film, DVDs, music CDs and videos, merchandising, magazines, books, theme parks, perfume, accessories, and clothes.

Celebrities are arguably the perfect vessels for an era of media convergence and transnational promotional synergies since they perform in multimedia contexts seamlessly moving between film, television, music, photography, gaming, and radio consumption contexts. They can advertise and sponsor any number of products and services in or through these multiple media channels, and they can work across any number of media platforms within a singular transnational media corporation's wide range of operations or relationships. One can link such celebrity cross-branding to the concept of the commodity fetish.

Smoking Lana Del Rey

Celebrities can be seen to be the very embodiment of what Karl Marx (1981) referred to as commodity fetishism, and celebrity culture can be reasoned to be the engine of the mystification of social relations in relation to production and consumption. The celebrity is a commodity fetish, and the work put into them to engineer their beauty, their idealism, and their perfected lifestyles is effaced so they appear natural or authentic. At the same time as commodity bodies, endowed with aura or charisma, they are turned into mystical or enchanted things. Their labour, and the labour of those involved in their manufacture, is removed from the signification chain and the production lines they are connected to. It is as if they have innate economic value; are of value in and of themselves; and that they exist in a magical state of commodity being in the world that makes invisible the alienated labour that went into making them. As Sue Collins suggests in relation to Michael Jordan and Nike

> While Disney and other national brands are self-endorsed, the additional inculcation of celebrity into production in advanced capitalism allows for an analysis of commodity abstraction from two perspectives: the celebrity endorsement from a production standpoint and the consumption of cultural meaning attributed to the celebrity endorsement that is embodied in the commodity-sign. From a production standpoint, the Jordan endorsement is the product of a social and economic process: that is, years of labor by Jordan and countless others (teammates, opponents, coaches, PR specialists) plus enormous sums of capital to nurture and sustain his success. The payoff for advertisers is obviously how well the super sport hero can sell products. (2001:2)

The celebrity turns the products they promote and endorse into higher-order fetishised commodities. They transfer their own mystical and quasi-religious status onto objects already mystified. These products appear as if they are symbiotically connected to the celebrity, and the fetish doubles itself: growing out of the product and out from the celebrity. The celebrity commodity is enchanted, and becomes like a holy artefact since it is imbued with the iconistic qualities of the celebrity and the mystical properties of the commodity, binding its fetishised nature.

Lana Del Rey is an American indie pop star who draws upon literary, fashion, political, cinematic, and musical reference points from post war America. She not only draws upon commodity intertexts, stands as a commodity, but she commodifies history, turning culture, her art, and history into an uber fetish. Del Rey's pop-inflected history is supernaturally affecting, effacing the decades of alienated labour, conflict, and impoverished value that has produced it all.

Del Rey's own stylised star-image draws upon Marilyn Monroe, Jackie Kennedy, Nancy Sinatra, Pricilla Presley, and to wider inter-textual references such as film noir, the femme fatale, the figure of the Lolita, and to fashion iconography of the late 1950s and 1960s. Her 'baked' long, full-bodied hair references high bouffant and beehive styles of the 1950s, while her voice and the string arrangements to her songs draws on vocal delivery and compositions from this period also, particularly the work of John Barry. Del Rey, however, conjoins this with contemporary pop references, beats, and loops, and cultural and political allusions to street culture, and the Bush and Obama periods. History, then, becomes a form of critical nostalgia; a yearning for a past long gone, tempered with unease about the present, an unease nonetheless which flows into the remnants of the past as they are gathered up in her video work. In an interview (Nokes, 2011), in relation to the importance of Coney Island to her music, she says

> 'Yeah, of course!' she says excitedly. 'Coney Island is the perfect mixture of grandeur and desolate, barren land. To me, that's gorgeousness, not to mention the most popular vacation destination of 1932. People came from all over North America just to sit by the seaside. Now no one goes there. To me, that is interesting. That's what I like in music; that's what I like in film; that's why I like Antony and the Johnsons; that's why I like David Lynch'.

Del Rey's music videos are fragmented pieces of pastiche and kitsch, filmed through naturalistic black-and-white photography or sepia tones, or a colour chromatic that signifies photography from a past age, from 16-mm home video footage, or from public footage she inserts herself into.

Each of her music videos are haunted by death, whether it is her own, the ones she causes; the death of a loved one or of love itself; the death of a celebrity image; or the death of the American dream. Del Rey places herself into, gleaming white trash or trailer park narratives (*Video Games*), iconic heterotropic spaces such as the aforementioned Coney Island, as well to the grandeur of the Kennedy's holiday house (*National Anthem*), or to opulent palaces where she is a fatalistic Queen (*Born to Die*). She is shot in brooding, enigmatic poses, and is involved in sexualised narratives of devotion, desire, and doomed love, where she is the object of the gaze and returns it, in heightened scenes of melancholy and sexual tension. Taken together, her video work turns objects, things, spaces, people into doom laden, enchanted commodity spectacles, which is

> The principle of commodity fetishism, the domination of society by 'intangible as well as tangible things', which reaches its absolute

fulfilment in the spectacle, where the tangible world is replaced by a selection of images which exist above it, and which simultaneously impose themselves as the tangible par excellence. (Debord, 1977: 36)

In the video to *National Anthem*, Del Rey plays Jacqueline Onassis, to black rapper A$AP Rocky's John F. Kennedy. The video begins with Del Rey performing as Marilyn Monroe in a re-enactment of her 1962 'Happy Birthday, Mr President' tribute. The scene ends with a reverse shot of Rocky as Kennedy, disrupting the expected racial classification, and setting in motion the collapse of linearity and the reinterpretation of American history. Del Rey is a vampish Monroe, a femme fatale, while Rocky repositions Kennedy as a gansta-style negro, replete with gold jewellery and rap iconography. He exists in the slipstream of hip-hop, black urbanism, and Obama, while Del Rey conjures up the murky death of Monroe. Together they insert themselves into a period of hopeful American history subsequently bloodied by Kennedy's assassination, the Watts race riots, Vietnam, and with it the overriding sense of the loss of innocence. The signifiers used, however, are hackneyed and cliché, built out of gender and racial stereotypes and the reincarnation of spectacle events, reconstructed through fetish imagery. Race is just a commodity to trade in a pimp aesthetic. Elis Cashmore suggests that soul-and-pop singer sensation Beyoncé also commodifies race

There is an ethos that she promotes: it is that racism may yet not be eradicated, but its effects can be nullified, not by confronting it, but by ignoring it and involving oneself in a life that emphasizes impulse rather than calculation, profligacy rather than thrift, the individual rather than society. (2010: 143)

The *National Anthem* video is then made up of re-enactments of famous scenes from the Kennedy's home movies, and of the Zapruder film of J. F. Kennedy's assassination. This bookends the music video, so that Kennedy dies, lives, and dies again, with Del Rey's Onassis providing the pathetic point of view through a colour de-saturated montage of their happiest times together. This montage is set against a backdrop of sumptuous imagery, a pouting Onassis sitting in front of a lion's skin; perfect children sitting on a green lawn with the ocean behind them; blurry rose gardens; and abstracted sexual chemistry and intimate looks and touching between her and Kennedy.

Kennedy's death in this film, however, has the buried echo of drive by shootings, or of a murder committed because of race and racial miscegenation. The music video inserts a new set of tensions into this well documented historical period but does so through a series of tangible and intangible spectacles, turning the principles players into commodity fetishes, broken stereotypes, confirming Del Rey as a celebrity commodity fetish, who enchants history, simplifies it, reincarnates it through fashion accessories, allusions to pop culture, and movie dream making.

In this translation of the star-celebrity, the metronome is itself a fetish, set to regulate and time the circulation and consumption of commodities endorsed by the celebrity fetish. The supernatural metronome turns time, the time of the celebrity, cultural time, into a plasma-like fetish, held over all things, that denies the time and value of labour, promoting the inherent worth in shiny things, so that all time (and space) becomes enchanted, willing slave to the master commodity. The celebrity metronome puts a spell on consumption so that it seems to magically just happen and will continue to happen forever and always.

What is also at work here is the cult of pseudo individuality. Del Rey positions herself as unique, representing uniqueness, her lyrical mandate a call to freeing individuality. The promotional work describe her as an 'organic upstart' (*Billboard*, January 2012), or as a 'bombshell singer-songwriter (who) blows up the blogs with songs about love, loss and video games' (*Rolling Stone*, 10 November 2011). However, she has been very carefully marketed as such, her star-image carefully planned after a failed early attempt at musical success as Lizzy Grant (her real name). Her difference is limited, her individuality a sham, she works within what Adorno and Horkheimer call the cultural industries through which identity is manufactured but passed off as unique

> From the standardized jazz improvisation to the exceptional film star whose hair curls over her eye to demonstrate her originality. What is individual is no more than the generality's power to stamp the accidental detail so firmly that it is accepted as such. The defiant reserve or elegant appearance of the individual on show is mass-produced like Yale locks, whose only difference can be measured in fractions of millimeters. The peculiarity of the self is a monopoly commodity determined by society; it is falsely represented as natural. (1979: 154)

Del Rey takes her mysterious star-image to fashion. She appeared on the cover of *Vogue* in March 2012 dressed in Louis Vuitton clothes and tagged as the 'fascinating Lana Del Rey'. She has had a retro-styled Mulberry bag named after her and was announced as the new face of fashion chain *H&M* in July 2012.

For her first fashion shoot for H&M, shot by the renowned haute couture photographers Inez van Lamsweerde and Vinoodh Matadin,

Del Rey wears a pale pink angora blend sweater and similarly coloured tight fitting jeans. Her hair is bouffant styled, her eyes are made up with heavy black eyeliner, her nails are long and sharp, and she has chandelier earrings dangling from her ears. In one of the photographs we see her side on, her hands placed on her cheek and forehead, her infinity hand tattoo visible, her eyes fixed on us. In another, a long shot, face on, we see one hand on the top of her thigh, the other on top of that, her nails sharp and her fingers elongated. The earrings and the long nails recall the fetishes used to eroticise the femme fatale of film noir. In fact, H&M's creative director, Donald Schneider, describes her look as 'very LA noir'. As a sultry, enigmatic, sad songstress she is a star-celebrity commodity fetish, wrapped in the material of dark fatale fetishes, promoting a fashion chain that is built on the mystique of fashion and the female form as a fetish. The commodity fetish doubles, grows, quadruples, magically, wrapped in the warm body of Lana del Rey.

One can argue, then, that the celebrity commodity fetish also works in relation to identity politics, particularly in terms of race and ethnicity. I would now like to explore the way that celebrity whiteness carries the higher orders of the commodity fetish in the contemporary world. To do this I will explore the idealised whiteness of Cate Blanchett.

The Miracle of Cate Blanchett

When a perfected star-image and idealised whiteness are combined, or brought together in symbiotic union, they construct a powerful narrative about privilege and belonging in the world, one that places or situates white identity at the apex of civilised and successful life. This idea of perfected identity in an enchanted world is achieved through suggesting that one can achieve the lifestyle and higher-order values of the idealised white star through consuming (their) products, many of which are suggested to be transformatory in nature. These products allow the consumer to become white, in and through the way they are possessed and re-materialised in the very act of taking in whiteness.

Film stars are mythological constructs, their narratives of success built on an imagined relationship with high order qualities and attributes. For example, the star success myth posits that film stars have a particularly close connection with the 'extraordinary' and the heavenly precisely because they are naturally more spiritual, are naturally closer to the heavens, precisely because they are made out of or from natural light. Film stars glow; they emit light and sunshine like no other human beings on earth. There is an aura around them that surrounds them, and which light up our dreary worlds too. They shine. However, as I will go onto discuss below, they are often suggested to shine through the consumer products they use, and that we should use if we want to be like them.

Further, the star success myth posits that perfected film stars are made in God's enlightened image, are, at least in a metaphorical sense, God's ideal(ised) and favoured children: the beautiful and the pure ones. In fact, some star images are as close to the Western pictorial idealisation of Jesus Christ as one can get. Warner E. Sallman's mass-reproduced twentieth-century painting of Jesus, *Head of Christ*, 'consistently depicted Christ with flowing, wavy, fair hair and light complexion' (Dyer, 1997: 68) and one can see such iconicity reproduced in the promotional stills of a young Robert Redford or Leonardo di Caprio, for example. In short, the star success myth locates the highest qualities of stardom *in* idealised forms of whiteness, so that they become synonymous with one another. Consumers gravitate towards this light, to the promise of enlightenment, seduced into buying substances and products that promise them such inner spiritual and outer physical liberation.

This is especially true in relation to white female stars, where the qualities of idealised whiteness – light, purity, and transcendence – seem to exude from their very pores, their inner state of being. Here, the 'non-physical, spiritual, indeed ethereal qualities' of the 'white woman as angel' (Dyer, 1997: 127) becomes transposed, or indexicaly grafted, on to the female star so that whiteness and stardom conjoin to produce a truly extraordinary and highly desirable representation that appears to-be-not-of, or rather, out-of-this-world. The white female star is supernatural, the perfect fetish.

Here though lies an apparent representational contradiction: in this coalescing sign system, the idealised white female star floats between being the ultimate object of identification, someone who is to be desired, and a subject who nonetheless remains above and beyond easy identification and sexual availability. *She* is 'embodied' in a state of being and not being, as someone who *miraculously* descends from the heavens with her virginity, purity intact, and yet one who simultaneously occupies the space of reproductive perfection. She is an impossible figure, but the impossibility of her promises redemption and reincarnation since one can embody her without being disembodied. In Jude Davies's textured analysis of Princess Diana he observes how the 'kindergarten' photograph of Diana worked in/through these tropes to represent her as the ultimate icon of idealised whiteness

Clearly, the terms in which Diana is produced here as ideal (white) female depend upon privileging reproduction and maternity as most desirable female activities, while keeping them totally separate from sexuality. Interlocking with this was the symbolic elaboration of Diana as what Anthony Burgess termed 'an icon of cleanliness'. As such, her lived experience of gendered identity was effaced by symbolically feminised discourses of Innocence, Chastity and Virtue. (2001: 154)

Where does cleanliness come from? It is from the domestic and beauty products that promise a home, a face, and a body free of dirt, blight, and imperfection. These products are not only about absences but ensuring the presence of idealised whiteness that will makes one's home ideal, and one's spiritual and physical self the very best it can be. When such products are endorsed or promoted by idealised white stars, whiteness becomes a commodity fetish ensuring its cultural, political, and economic power.

Cate Blanchett is an idealised white star, a perfected image of female whiteness, naturally, inescapably so, or so she is imagined to be. However, she advertises SK-II beauty products by suggesting whiteness is something that can be bought and then transformed by. One can become ideally white – possess Blanchett's beauty – if one purchases the products she says she uses. Blanchett can be located as a hyper-white star who carries idealised values such as purity, youthfulness, idealised femininity, and a higher class position, that together give her social standing and a desiring and desirable position from which to enunciate from. Blanchett glows in these SK-II adverts, she is imagined to have an inner light which is marked as essential to her (to whiteness), and which grants her access to identity positions that empower her, and whiteness as a subject position. While whiteness remains invisible as a racial category in these adverts, it nonetheless shapes the streams of representation that Blanchett is found in, its invisibility a central part of its power to define the ideal and the idealised.

The form of idealised female whiteness as embodied by Blanchett is a 'miracle' and as such has religious and transcendent undertones that cannot or shouldn't be questioned. She *is* an aura of perfected female whiteness, seemingly beyond reproductive markers. These adverts also play out something of the transnational, suggesting her idealised whiteness is the property of global relationships, and the material out of which 'lost' identities can be re-made.

In the first television advert for the *SK-II Pitera Essence Range* (Japan/ Australia 2011), Blanchett introduces the viewer to 'the miracle' of the product. Filmed in a verdant green bamboo forest, Blanchett is the personification and embodiment of idealised whiteness, her blonde hair, natural pale skin, and long, flowing white dress the signifiers of this racial purity and perfection. Her face is intermittently captured in close-up, with soft, suffuse lighting creating the impression of a natural halo around her shoulders. Her hair flutters in the wind as she glides through the forest, translucent-like, barely touching the ground she walks on. Blanchett appears at one with nature, naturally, essentially white.

Blanchett is nature and yet she is also culture/cultured, the embodiment of civilised life, a connection metaphorically made in the way the scene cuts to an image of the product in a white laboratory where its ingredients appear like milk, and then composed from clear, clean water. The qualities and values of the product and the qualities and values of Blanchett are being shared and approximated – she is milk also, she is an icon of cleanliness.

The voice-over that she delivers adds a soft aural tone to the imagery, supported by non-diegetic music that calls upon traditional Japanese arrangement. Blanchett tells us 'I have been using SK-II for nine years now on this path to crystal clear skin'. This autobiographical narration is a dizzy mixture of allusions and associations drawing upon Western enlightenment rhetoric, and Buddhist/Taoist philosophy, while linking it to the very best techno-scientific linguistic naming practices – this is a product that has gone through at least 11 different iterations to get to this level of perfection. Blanchett, the product, is engaged in a journey that leads to (or sustains) idealised white perfection. This is a journey to enlightenment we can all take if only we use the cream.

Idealised whiteness is imagined to be youthful – wrinkle-free and auratic in its shine. This youthfulness is the elixir of the perfected self; it is what we should all aspire to be like. We learn that the secret ingredients for the product came through the recognition that the hands that were used in the preparation for sake appeared youthful, although the image of the Japanese hands that is supplied looks both wrinkle-free and whiter than the rest of the body. Race is being effaced or made safe at the exact same time it is being foregrounded and orientalised. We are introduced to the idea of tactility and cross-modality; these Japanese hands become the face made over, in an oriental slave to white master or mistress like relationship. The association works subtextualy, of course, but the link to Blanchett who has her face attended to by make-up artists and the like, for all manner of photo shoots and film work, connects the mythic signifiers together.

The advert suggests that the qualities and perfections of whiteness is ultimately attainable through this product, or more complexly, that one can have a relationship with 'natural' Japanese environs, ingredients, and products and become idealised white in the process. Of course, it is white techno science that has turned these raw ingredients into something potent and safe to use. This is the miracle that Blanchett, the product, offers the consumer, wherever they may live: the ability to pass or rather become hyper-white through the re-engineering of nature, of *Other* cultures, and of whiteness itself.

In the period between 2011 and 2012 there has been a 'shiro nuri' (white painting) trend amongst Lolita and gothic subcultures in Japan, centred on the idea of 'seiyou kabure' or those who admire European history and European culture. Such a trend can be read as a desire to look Western (separate from the white face tradition of the geisha). Although SK-II is being aimed in this advert at 30-plus, middle class women in Australasia, it may well also be tapping into this white face-painting trend in Japan but for older Japanese women. However, rather than a make-up, which can be washed off, it is moisture that transforms the skin, making it lighter, younger looking, implicitly whiter. Images of whiteness circulate freely and widely in the digital, virtual age but they are made to be as culturally invisible as 'the cloud' that our information is increasingly stored in.

On the SK-II website Blanchett is described as the product's global ambassador. The use of the word ambassador is notable, presenting her as one who is championing a cause, often used when a celebrity is associated with an organisation or pressure group committed to political, environmental, and cultural change in some way. Here her role is to promote how successful the range is in making her skin 'even toned' and 'how it seemed to glow'. That word glow again, glowing across the international footprints of the SK-II website, glowing into Asia, Europe, and North America. Whiteness made virtual but embodied, the ultimate commodity fetish that one can possess regardless of race or ethnicity, shining out across the globe today. Buy some.

The Celebrity Ambassador

What also glows or flows across the international borders is the development work undertaken by celebrities; the charity and campaign work they are involved in; the causes they attach their name too; the aid agencies they work for; the protests they attend; and the activism that marks out their ethical beliefs and values. Whether it be Brad Pitt's Make it Right Foundation, a nonprofit organisation committed to the financing and building of 150 new houses in New Orleans' Ninth Ward, devastated by flooding; *Green Day* donating all royalties from the iTunes sales of their single 'Boulevard of Broken Dreams' to help victims of the 2010 Asian tsunami through the International Red Cross; Mia Farrow's role as a UNICEF goodwill ambassador and campaigner for children's' rights; or Andy Murray being a founding member of the *Malaria No More* UK Leadership Council, celebrities across all fields are connected to local, national, and international development campaigns. When it comes to the category of supporting disadvantaged and dispossessed children, for example, there are 1830 celebrities attached to 576 charities (see http://www.looktothestars.org/cause for a full list). As Goodman and Barnes contends

> Celebrities are quickly becoming the new face of charities, foundations and activists campaigns, and as we have it more broadly here, 'development', as the voice of the oppressed and down-trodden Other for a global, very often female, consuming audience. (2010: 4)

The question of why celebrities are involved in development work and why development agencies, aid organisations and protest groups look to have celebrity ambassadors attached to them, can be answered through reference to branding, value transference, and cross promotion activities. The celebrity in identifying with a just cause, an urgent need, a long-term deserving project is hoping to see it impact upon how they are viewed by the media, their fans, and consumers. Development work humanises and moralises the celebrity. It also enables those who are seen to have ascribed fame to be reinterpreted or resignified as having achieved fame, since their heroic pursuit of social transformation is a way of validating their (undeserved) success status. For example, 'train wreck' celebrity Lindsay Lohan took part in the BBC Three documentary, *Lindsay Lohan's Indian Journey* (April 2010), to demonstrate her inner ethical purposefulness. As the promotional blurb suggests

> Hollywood actress Lindsay Lohan travels to India to investigate the issue of child trafficking. As the capital Delhi prepares to host the Commonwealth Games, she talks to young boys just rescued from factories in the slums. When she learns that many have been sent away with traffickers by their own parents, Lindsay sets off to find out why. In West Bengal, parents, child victims, and a former trafficker share their stories and reveal the desperate poverty which fuels this cruel trade in children. As India's economy is booming, Lindsay

asks what can be done to stop this abuse. (http://www.bbc.co.uk/programmes/b00rvbtl)

Lohan's journey is not meant to be just a physical one, but an inner transformation, an awakening of the self, and the politicisation of her hitherto designation as a toxic celebrity. Of course, in the age of cross-media promotion, BBC Three is also being branded as ethical, as being part of the healing and transformation process the world needs, and as capable of attracting a star like Lohan to its network.

In terms of identification processes and wider ideological import, the heroic journey that Lohan takes is supposed to resonate with fans and viewers, and create an individualised sense of moral responsibility – that the individual has the power to effect change. Celebrity ambassadors lead the way, show us the light, and create a culture for giving at the individual level that allows us to believe we are making a difference.

We make a difference in the shadow of people we greatly admire, confirming them as care givers of the world, while at the same time having conferred on us a sense of duty that belongs within a just political and economic capitalist system (masking the disadvantage and exploitation that cries out for systematic change). As Goodman and Barnes contend:

> The celebritisation of development has worked to turn 'development' as a wider project into one that is individualized, volunteerised, privatised, and, ultimately responsibilised onto audiences, consumers, and citizens (mostly of the North) as more celebrities take o their roles as endorsers of campaigns and causes. The 'heroic individual' in the form of the celebrity ... is now here to exalt us into doing something as 'caring' individual, much like they are doing, by giving to a cause, organization or charity, shopping in a certain store or buying a certain (most likely fair traded) product. (2010:4)

Development agencies, charities, and aid networks employ celebrities because they help raise their national and international visibility, and cash, tools, and donations follow. The celebrity ambassador is very often equipped with performance skills that allow them to articulate, embody, and communicate what is at issue in terms of the cause or concern they support. They are intimately connected to the media chains and communication flows, and can guarantee radio, television, and newspaper coverage if they step off a plane somewhere. Celebrities sell charity very well.

On the 4 April 2012, UNICEF goodwill ambassador Mia Farrow met in Chad with refugees from Darfur waiting to go home. We are told she, 'listened to their stories', 'has visited Chad many times', and 'speaks with 9-year-old Bakhit in the Koubigou displacement camp, near Goz Beïda, Chad. Bakhit was seriously injured by a landmine'. She reunites with an 'old friend' whom we learn she first 'met in 2006. She had just come, her village had been destroyed and she was in a very emotional frame of mind. It was among the worst years of the violence, and people were still coming in from Darfur'.

Farrow is photographed sitting amongst the female refugees, as if she is both one of them and a councillor who can listen to and help assuage their pain. She holds a baby close, becomes a transnational mother figure (Farrow has adopted 9 dispossessed children, we learn from her own website). She is dressed in everyday clothes, jeans, and a long-sleeved UNICEF t-shirt, and her hair is in pigtails, to keep it both off the face and to help feminise her. She cares deeply, is the message, and has been willed into action time and time again on the behalf of displaced mothers and their (*our*) children everywhere. Thus, Farrow displays an 'extraordinary ordinariness', one that could match our ordinary extraordinariness if only we go in search of it, are willed into action to do so.

Farrow is also an activist and this requires a rather different form of celebrity embodiment. Farrow co-founded the 'Dream for Darfur' campaign that attempted to put pressure on the Chinese government to influence the Sudanese government into letting international police into its country to stop the levels of violence there. For the 2008 Olympics Farrow led an unofficial torch relay in Hong Kong at the same time as the official Olympic torch relay was taking place. She delivered a speech calling on world leaders to boycott the 2008 Summer Olympics opening ceremony and criticising the corporate sponsors of the Olympics for not pressuring China on Darfur. During the Olympics, Farrow televised via the Internet from a Sudanese refugee camp to highlight China's involvement in the region. Her activism is also a type of brand; it relies on her celebrity image; her 'charity' work with UNICEF; and her own promotional work that keeps her in the media eye.

Whether activism or ambassadorial in form, one can read the performance of do-good celebrities in terms of event spectacle that creates 'superstars' of those involved (Kellner, 2003). *Live 8*, BBC's *Children in Need*, are image seductive, sentimental, and involve a highly visualised staging crafted out of the techniques and strategies of commodity and corporate branding. This can involve styling the celebrity over a number of years so that they faithfully embody the cause they are attached to. For example, Angelina Jolie auditioned to be a celebrity ambassador

> Her links with UNHCR were established over several years in which she 'auditioned' to become a Goodwill Ambassador. Jolie became acquainted with the plight of refugees through trips to West Africa, and has used her photogenic qualities to attract the attention of world's media. Similarly, UNHCR has sought to place 'attractive' refugees in the camera frame next to her to provide an iconic representation of displacement. (Tsaliki, Frangonikolopoulos, and Huliaras, 2011: 56)

In these charity extravaganzas, celebrity egos are being emotionalised. Heartstrings pulled. Emotion is being turned into a star-spangled high-event fetish. Careers are being re-staged in the atrophic light of philanthropic generosity and kindness. Help is at hand. Change is going to come. Change is not going to come.

No Business Like Political Business

Contemporary politicians are a type of celebrity and they work in the arena of 'show business'. Each meaningful, telegenic celebrity politician is styled, coached, scripted, and trained for their life in front of the lens. One can read their journey up the political ladder as a series of auditions for bigger parts, for more air-time, and for a stronger self-centred, goal-oriented brand that voters and corporate sponsors will buy into. The public arenas we find them in, the speeches they give, the dinners they attend, and the advertorial work they do to raise finance and push a policy occur through the mechanisms and practices of celebrity spectacle and commodity consumption. As Doug Kellner summarises

> With the increasing tabloidization of corporate journalism, lines between news, information and entertainment have blurred, and politics has become a form of entertainment and spectacle. Candidates enlist celebrities in their election campaigns and are increasingly covered in the same way as celebrities, with tabloidised news obsessing about their private lives. In this context, presidential candidates themselves become celebrities and are packaged and sold like the products of the culture industry. (2009: 715)

US President Barack Obama is a super political brand built upon a mandate of change and transformation. His 2008 Presidential campaign was focused on creating a new and improved political and ideological product that weary American voters could believe in. This 'change is going to come' product was showcased in bumper college rallies, glitzy electoral speeches, campaign trails, television talk shows, advertorial YouTube videos, and the social media through which Obama images and slogans could be relayed and replayed over and over again. Obama slogans such as 'Change we can believe in', 'It's about Time. It's about Change', 'I'm asking you to believe not just in my ability to bring about real change in Washington. I'm asking you to believe in yours', and 'a new beginning', are exactly like advertorial copy

> Found in advertisements for everything from weight-loss products ('a new you') to fizzy drinks. In fact, Obama's campaign slogans resemble or replay Pepsi Cola's (1984–91) 'Pepsi. The choice of a new generation', and 2008/9 'Something for everyone' and 'Every generation refreshes the world'. In terms of the social networking sites Obama was intent on hitting, the slogans not only fit the reduced format perfectly but also echo the way in which celebrities write themselves online and through mobile technologies. For example, Miley Cyrus sloganises: 'Find ur voice; take action; change ur world'. (Redmond, 2010: 88)

The news and magazine coverage that followed Obama made a celebrity spectacle out of him, positioning him in the same way as auratic individuals from the film, entertainment and film industries. In Vanity Fair's *Special Commemorative Inauguration Issue* (2008), Obama is photographed in the same pose as a film star, staring enigmatically back at the camera, as we imagine him contemplating the future as an actor might contemplate a role. Directly running across the picture (the body) of Obama runs two closely proximate bylines, 'The Obama Era Begins!' and 'Plus: Hollywood 2009'. The symbolic connection here, that Obama is made in and of the Hollywood dream factory, cannot be lost. Political philosophy and policy become washed in the same soap powder, the same melodramatic soap opera; Obama promotes health care in the same way Blanchett sells facial cream. The journey they both speak of is one of enlightenment through dream making, illusion, and the commodification of life, love, and politics. Dream on, and be touched by the messages they convey.

Touch Me

Celebrities touch us both in the metaphoric sense and in the lived and living sense of feeling them in our hearts, desires, and longings. We feel them deeply, as carnal creatures that impress on our own carnality. They can arouse us, make us cry; move us to action and reaction. They invite us to cluster around them in fan groups and through events that ask us to respond to them through heightened emotion, through screaming, chanting, and sensorial excess. While these engagements are clearly orchestrated around consumption processes and practices, as this chapter has demonstrated; while auratic commodity intertexts circulate freely; and while one can see these emotional interactions as parasocial and ideological, identification with the celebrity cannot be ultimately reduced to such mechanical frames.

At a live concert, when girls swoon for Justin Bieber, or young lovers huddle together to feel in their shared hearts the emotional strings of Del Ray, they are not thinking about ticket prices, they are not lost in the world of commodity dreaming. Rather, they are feeling the celebrity as a celebaesthetic being, sensing them as they sense themselves in a carnal exchange not reducible to words, not accountable simply to the operations of liquid capitalism. The body opens itself in these encounters, is less docile and regulated often, love gushes out of it, an opening of transgressive and liberating desires takes place. While this liberation of the senses may be short-lived, may ultimately be recuperated in the services of patriarchy and consumption, there is nonetheless moments in time and space where the body is free, and where the celebrity metronome is let loose.

Lana Del Rey (honey, rose petals, sex, nostalgia, American Beauty, pink plastic).

4 Selling Celebrity

I am at the supermarket on a bleak Saturday morning. Adele's Rolling in the Deep is playing on the store's speaker system, her voice flooding the aisles. For the past few months, although it seems much, much longer, Adele has been the constant soundtrack to everyday life. Her music has taken over radio station playlists, and has blasted out in shopping malls, gyms, lifts, fashion shops, bars and restaurants, sports arenas, wedding bashes, birth parties, birthday parties, and retirement get-togethers. Her songs have become the beat of the aural celebrity metronome, sold and bought in their millions. Adele is for sale everywhere, and capitalism can't be tamed.

One Direction

One can define the production and circulation of celebrity as a synergetic, transnational industry involving a set of commercial processes with the aim of profit-making. Celebrities can be argued to be manufactured in the same way as other goods and services, with techniques of renewal and transformation to ensure commodity longevity. At the same time the celebrity industry is involved in the constant churning out of new faces with a limited life span, ensuring an endless stream of profit possibilities from those that role off the production line.

Manufactured teen bands and idols, including those that emerge from television 'talent' formats, often have a two- to three-year cycle of success that runs first from their mediated launch or the length of the series, to the release of the first single and album, and subsequent live tours. Near the end of the period of time they are saleable, another new band will be launched, or another new talent series will have been aired. The turn to the manufacture of the ordinary celebrity that appear on television formats such as *Big Brother* is seen to speed up this process of relentless commodity renewal. As Graeme Turner suggests

Among the consequences of the trend towards the ordinary celebrity and the success of reality TV formats is an acceleration of the
industrial cycle of use and disposal for the products of these trends.
If performing on *Big Brother* can generate celebrity within a matter of
days, it can disappear just as quickly. Indeed, it is essential that each
crop of Big Brother housemates are easily replaced by the next if the
format is to successfully reproduce itself, series after series. In this
regard, television's production of celebrity can truly be regarded as
a manufacturing process into which the product's planned obsoles-
cence is incorporated. The replaceable celebrity-commodity (Turner,
Bonner, and Marshall David, 2000: 12–13) is structurally fundamental
to both of the leading primetime formats aimed at the key 14–35 year
old demographics: reality TV and soap opera. (2006: 155)

At the suggestion of guest judge Nicole Scherzinger, teen pop band *One
Direction* were formed during the 7th series of the UK's music talent
show, *The X-Factor*. Having first failed as solo contestants, as a constituted group they were easily packaged and marketed to tweens and teens
as the perfect blend of romantic heartthrobs and ethnically 'diverse'
heterosexual Adoni. As Stephanie Abrahams (2012) writes, 'each member
has his own shtick: Horan is the "cute little Irish one", Malik is the "quiet
and mysterious one", Payne is "the sensible one", Styles is "the charming
one", and Tomlinson is "the funny one"'. Each persona, nonetheless, is
but a marketable entity that signifies individuality but whose difference
is a commercial sham so that fans can choose a favourite to invest in.
As Horan, Malik, Payne, Styles, and Tomlinson grow older, as another
new pop idol or boy band comes along to replace them, and as their fans
grow older (grow up), the mass manufacturing, industrial process will
continue.

Simon Cowell immediately saw the band's potential, and signed
them up to his record label Syco for a reported $2 million. Syco's parent
company is Sony Music Entertainment, which also own Columbia
Records and which struck a deal with the band to distribute their
records in North America. Such cross-media ownership ensures that
they would be bought and sold in the world marketplace. A series of
big event marketing and promotion opportunities were organised,
including the *X-Factor* Live Tour; a sold-out 62-venue world tour; an
appearance in the United States on *The Today Show* at the Rockefeller
Centre, in front of an estimated 15,000 fans; Brit Award appearances (to
perform and collect an award); a slot on the closing night of the London
Olympics; endorsement work for Pokémon and Nokia; and a global toy

line with Hasbro. As Nick Gatfield, chairman and chief executive officer of Sony Music Entertainment UK, stated, 'What you might not know about *One Direction* is that they already represent a $50 million business and that's a figure we expect to double next year'.

To launch and promote their new Up All Night live concert DVD, *One Direction* held a global Twitter viewing party at 5.30 p.m. BST on the 31 May 2012:

> Harry, Niall, Zayn, Liam and Louis will be pressing play on their DVD player and watching along to Up All Night – The Live Tour. Music week reports, 'using the hashtag #1DVDWatchParty, the band will tweet about their favourite moments, as well as sharing behind-the-scenes stories and gossip'. Whilst interacting with viewers, the group members will be 'adding fellow viewers to their follow list and retweeting their favourite comments'.

The promotional activity here is meant to be like a shared screening of the film, in a domestic space, on the couch in front of the TV, with the boys present. A shared and interactive conversation is being suggested also, with the DVD viewing experience a memento, a keepsake, with favourite moment memories replayed. Multiple concrete and abstract commodities are in production here; tweeting; brand loyalty; the DVD; the records and future concert tickets; and ancillary merchandising embedded in the DVD and found in the shops, and on their official website. This event functions as a shop window for all that they sell, where fans can buy the live concert DVD in their home currency.

According to Rein, Kotler, and Stoller (1997: 42–58), the celebrity industry is served by, or is an amalgamation of, the following sub-industries, each of which can be seen to be intimately tied to the way *One Direction* were manufactured. First, there is the entertainment industry, which includes the spaces of performance and reception including theatres, cinemas, film studios, dance halls, and sports arenas. These are spaces of spectacle, cinematic and telegenic in setting and delivery, where crowds flock to see and be seen. *One Direction*'s performance at the closing of the 2012 Olympic Games would be an example of spectacular enchantment, of pure 'show business'.

Second, there is the communications industry, which includes the production of magazines, newspapers, radio, Internet interfaces, mobile phones, and film and television. In the past 12 months, between 2011 and 2012, *One Direction* has occupied central spaces in all of these communications media, often in tandem with performances produced by the entertainment industry. For example, on 22 August 2011 the BBC released a 'One Direction Top of the Pops' magazine special edition that included three giant posters, two cute door handles, and 12 cute posters. This preceded by three weeks the release of their debut single, *What Makes You Beautiful*, which entered the UK charts at number 1. *One Direction* appeared on BBC Radio Ulster's, the Alan Simpson show, on the 20 August 2011, to perform *What Makes You Beautiful*. They also appeared on the BBC Breakfast show on the 17 November 2011, and opened the call for donations on the *BBC Children In Need Appeal Night Live* on Friday 18 November 2011. All these entertainment performances, through communication channels, were organised by agents and agencies working for the public relations industries.

Third, then there is the publicity industry comprised of public relations agencies and companies, publicists, advertising agencies, marketing research companies, event planners, and brand managers. The publicity industry is involved in a range of activities including brand planning and integrated marketing strategies; maintaining brand identity and awareness; market research and evaluation; promotions, product tie-ins and endorsement opportunities; the writing and editing of press releases, articles, speeches, scripts, and publications; special event planning and organisation; issue and crisis management; press agentry; and counselling those they represent on how to handle the media and best represent themselves when in the public eye. According to the IPR Australia, the aim of public relations is 'the deliberate, planned and sustained effort to establish and maintain mutual understanding between an organisation and its publics'. What is not acknowledged in this definition is that 'mutual understanding' is organised in the service of sales and profitability.

If one was to apply this definition to celebrity one would see PR creating an environment where the celebrity is seen favourably by the entertainment and communications industries (public one), fans and consumers (public two), and wider community and civil groups (public three), with the overall aim of inter-promotional opportunities, song, tour and album sales, and merchandising tie-ins. On all three counts, *One Direction* has been positively positioned; they enjoy supportive coverage in the press, radio, and television; have a large and loyal fan base; and they have begun to be invited to perform at spectacle events such as the London Olympics 2012. *One Direction* is represented by UK-based entertainment PR agency HJPR who also have as their clients, *Ant and Dec, Dannii Minogue, Boys II Men,* and the *X-Factor Finalists 2011* and *X-Factor Live Tour 2012* – all of these acts are also linked to Simon Cowell and Syco Entertainment. HJPR describe their work as

A small and dedicated team of professionals passionate about our work, we work closely with the UK's leading management companies, record labels and TV channels. With our methods constantly evolving along with the rapidly changing PR landscape, we execute proactive campaigns promoting specific projects, as well as 24/7 reactive media profile management. Simply put, we provide clients with the best strategic advice and media contacts in the entertainment industry. PR and publicity is a vital part of any artist's career. Responsible for breaking and sustaining the careers of many leading acts, HJPR believe Print Media, Online and Broadcast should all work seamlessly together to achieve the highest impact results.

This sense of seamless integration of commodity branding is imagined to occur with the entertainment and communication industries but also through the representation, appearance, and performance industries. Celebrities have personal managers and publicists who work with them on a day-to-day basis, who advise on how they should be represented and how they should represent themselves; they have a number of image consultants who style their appearance; and they have a range of performance coaches and teachers who over the course of their careers help them speak, sing, dance, play, and act.

With *One Direction* this all initially took place within the talent-finding arena of *The X- Factor*. Representation, appearance transformation, and professional training were all taking place within the diegetic folds of the show: their makeover and development as artists were reflectively commented upon and demonstrated in developmental discourse through the comments of judges and those involved in coaching them. Key people who were to be involved in their career post-*The X-Factor* were involved in brand development while the shown was being run. As Graeme Turner suggests:

Installing ordinary people into game shows, docu-soaps and reality TV programming enables television to 'grow their own' celebrity, to control how they are marketed before, during and after production – all of this while still subordinating the celebrity of each individual to the needs of the particular programme or format. The extent to which this is now done, and the pervasive visibility its most successful products can achieve, make this is an extremely significant shift not only in terms of the production and consumption of celebrity but also in terms of how the media now participate in the cultural construction of identity and desire. (2006: 156)

The seventh industry is the endorsement industry involved in manufacturing souvenirs, clothes, products, and merchandising lines. At the onedirectionstore.com one can purchase One Direction huddies, T-shirts, CDs, DVDs, mugs, sunglasses, hot water bottles, tote bags, silly bands, rubber keyrings, posters, signed posters and photocard sets, tour programmes, collector sets, and a collectors iPhone set (which includes: 'One Direction iPhone 4 protective cover – simple snap on design and ultra slim fit featuring a full colour design. Phone charm including 3 tags featuring a full colour heart shaped band photo, heart 1D logo and silver coloured One Direction text. Double sided key chain featuring the 1D boys and Love 1D logo – perfect for your home of locker key!'). The merchandising around One Direction is meant to touch every facet of a fan's daily life. The desire for their products comes out of a desire to be close to them, to have them close to you, in your pocket, in your school bag, next to your heart.

The final industry is the legal and business services industry, which provides legal and financial advice. This advice centres on contracts, investments, copyright, tax matters, property, stocks and shares, and litigation matters. So central has lawyers become to the celebrity industry that there are celebrity lawyers, famous in the media, who represent celebrity clients. Lawyer Mark Geragos has a celebrity client list that includes Michael Jackson, Winona Ryder, Chris Brown, and Scott Peterson. However, his outspoken advocacy for his clients regularly places him in the public eye.

One Direction have been in a naming dispute with One Direction US, who claim they had filed a trademark application for their name before One Direction UK had performed on the X-Factor. In response, Simon Cowell/Syco filed a counter-claim, saying fans would be confused by the name similarity. The legal industry is here being aligned with the publicity industry not only through Syco fronting the legal case but because the situation demanded crisis management and media handling. What is being suggested in this case study is a concentration in market relations between these various sub-industries with wide cultural and societal consequences. Sarah Adams (2012) suggests that

> The media industry is a highly concentrated system of ownership performing under profit-driven logic within an oligopolical market structure. The concentration and conglomeration of media firms encourage production of content that will maximize industry profit. Media's concentrated ownership imposes pressures of corporate

capitalism, exploits overpowering affects of advertising, and generates media's ultimate externality, a hyper-commercialized society.

The celebrity metronome is the beat of a hyper-commercialised society, every moment of its swing connecting one media corporation to another; one product to another; one commodity or service to another; all under the spell of celebrities who embody their lust for profit, who cloak them in the fairy dust of magic kingdoms that we are seduced into wanting. If there is one media corporation that today sells celebrity to the world then it is the Walt Disney Company. One can read the operations of Walt Disney's celebrity production as a type of transmedia storytelling, and Miley Cyrus as one if its best cross-promotional characters.

The Miley Who Sold the World: Celebrity Transmedia Narratives

If one were to examine the operations of the Walt Disney Company one would see an integrated, synergetic behemoth with a revenue of \$40.1 billion for 2011. The company operates in five integrated markets: media networks, parks and resorts, studio entertainment, consumer products, and interactive media. For example, according to Reuters (2012) its media networks division is comprised of:

> International and domestic cable networks and its broadcasting business, which consists of a domestic broadcast television network, television production operations, domestic and international television distribution, domestic television stations, domestic and international broadcast radio networks, domestic radio stations, and publishing and digital operations.

Its Parks and Resorts division includes the Walt Disney World Resort in Florida, the Disneyland Resort in California, Aulani, a Disney Resort and Spa in Hawaii, the Disney Vacation Club, the Disney Cruise Line, and Adventures by Disney. The company has a stake of 51 per cent in Disneyland Paris, 47 per cent in Hong Kong Disneyland Resort, and 43 per cent in Shanghai Disney Resort. The company also licenses the operations of the Tokyo Disney Resort in Japan. The company's Walt Disney Imagineering unit designs and develops new theme park concepts and attractions as well as resort properties.

The Studio Entertainment division produces and acquires live-action and animated motion pictures, direct-to-video content, musical recordings, and live stage plays. The focus is on Disney-branded films under the Walt Disney Pictures and Pixar banners, and Marvel-branded films. The primary company titles for its films are Walt Disney Pictures, Touchstone Pictures, Pixar, Marvel, and Disneynature. According to Reuters (2012), as of 1 October 2011

> The Company had approximately 1,700 active produced and acquired titles, including 1,300 live-action titles and 400 animated titles, in the domestic home entertainment marketplace and approximately 2,900 active produced and acquired titles, including 2,400 live-action titles and 500 animated titles, in the international marketplace.

The Consumer Products division designs, develops, publishes, promotes, and sells a wide variety of products based on existing and new characters. These include toys, clothes, home decor and furnishings, stationery, accessories, jewellery, health and beauty products, novelty food, footwear, and electronics. Some of the items licensed by the Walt Disney include Mickey Mouse, the Disney Princess, Toy Story, the Lion King, Disney Fairies, Hannah Montana, and the Marvel franchise that includes Spider Man, Captain America, and Iron Man. Disney Publishing Worldwide (DPW) publishes children's books and magazines in multiple countries and languages including *Disney and Me* and *Disney Princess* magazine.

The Interactive Media Group division 'creates and delivers branded entertainment and lifestyle content across interactive media platforms' (Reuters, 2012). The primary focus is on producing multi-platform games for global distribution. The Games business creates, develops, markets, and distributes console and handheld games worldwide based on characters and stories created by the other divisions, including 2011 titles such as LEGO *Pirates of the Caribbean*, and *Cars 2*, and 2012 titles such as *Brave* and *The Avengers*. The Games business also produces online games, such as *Disney's Club Penguin* and *Disney Fairies Pixie Hollow*, interactive games for social networking websites such as *Gardens of Time*, and interactive games for smartphone platforms. Disney Online produces

> Kids and family-targeted entertainment through a portfolio of Websites including Disney.com and the Disney Family Network. Disney.com integrates many of the Company's Disney-branded

Internet sites including sites for the Disney Channel, Disney Parks and Resorts, Walt Disney Pictures and Disney Consumer Products. (Reuters, 2012)

The Walt Disney Company, then, is a way of life, a part of the cultural fabric of social and familial relations across the planet. What drives their output is celebrity figures, the culture of fame, and the myth of heroic individualism personified or anamorphosised through their animation figures or live-action stars, who populate their films, TV shows, and games.

Each of the company's divisions sell celebrity, promotes celebrity lifestyle, and conjures up happiness and belonging through the texts, goods, toys, parks, games, and consumer products that are constructed before the gaze of fame and fortune. One can examine this commodity celebrification of modern life as a series of transmedia celebrity narratives. In fact, one can think of the contemporary celebrity industry as producing celebrities to be transmedia story products who only make sense because of the way they move in and across a number of media texts, user platforms, and commodity and consumption contexts.

Henry Jenkins (2007) has defined contemporary media storytelling as involving ten cross-promotional and platform relationships. These can be usefully applied to the way celebrities are also types of cross-promotion, multi-platform stories, working within a celebrity-industrial matrix, which operates right across the media industries. I would like to take each of Jenkins's ten transmedia storytelling ingredients in turn, using Miley Cyrus/Hannah Montana as the case study to illustrate how they can best be seen as celebrity-inspired narratives.

1. *Transmedia storytelling represents a process where integral elements of a fiction get dispersed systematically across multiple delivery channels for the purpose of creating a unified and coordinated entertainment experience* (Jenkins, 2007).

Transmedia celebrities are fictive constructs whose images and stories get dispersed systematically across print, press, television, music, game, and virtual sites and networks. We understand celebrities as the sum parts of these textual fragments; as unified storied beings who grant and award us pleasure through the way we can see them in one platform advertising cologne or sneakers; in another, the subject of gossip and innuendo; in another, scoring a great goal or giving a stunning live music performance; in another, taking on the role of a narrative agent in a game; and in another, campaigning on behalf of cancer or hunger in Africa.

These integral narrative elements are the clues to the celebrity's entire social and moral universe: we can only understand them fully if we have full access to these stories. We only get full enjoyment of the celebrity if we consume them in and across these media platforms and sites.

Miley Cyrus became a celebrity through the Hannah Montana Disney television series (2006–2011), which lasted for four seasons. In it, she plays Miley Stewart/Hannah Montana, a normal teenage girl by day, a pop star by night. Hannah Montana spawned two movies: the first, *Hannah Montana & Miley Cyrus: Best of Both Worlds Concert* (Hendricks, 2008), is a live concert film from Walt Disney Pictures presented in Disney Digital 3-D. The self-reflexive character titling of Miley (Cyrus) as Miley (Stewart) in the show, and the live concert film that 'introduces' us to 'Miley Cyrus', begins to construct a homogeneous narrative – a star in the making, a star all along – from which her celebrity status will fully emerge.

Miley Cyrus is birthed as the celebrity embodiment of Hannah Montana, her fiction a core part of Miley's true self. Miley is signified as a southern Christian, a devoted family girl, a virgin until she will marry, but also a naturally talented singer, a pop star. She is 'extraordinary ordinary', and factualises the fiction of Hannah Montana. She is Miley Cyrus by day, pop sensation by night.

The elements of this narrative are found in magazine shoots, interviews, confessions, tweets, Facebook profiles, official web pages from 2006 until 2010, which is the point at which her personal celebrity narrative began to shift and Cyrus became sexualised. That there is progression and difference to these plots and stories help create and sustain the pleasure we get from her. Cyrus's second album, *Can't Be Tamed* (2010) presents a new dance-pop sound, and a more sexualised and vampish image.

The video for the single of the album's title has Cyrus trapped in a cage, a near 'extinct species'. She is leather clad, has a feathered plumage, and mid-way through the video escapes the cage (her adult sexuality, her *new* celebrity image) that she is being held and observed in. This is a narrative of her own celebrity image, an awakening of her adult sexual self, and a re-positioning of her identity. The release of the album coincided with news and magazines stories about drug taking and wild partying, and confessional tweets. For example, *MSN Video* posted (12 December 2010)

Exclusive: Miley Cyrus drugs scandal

Miley Cyrus is caught on camera by TMZ giggling uncontrollably after taking a hit on the pipe which is said to have been salvia, a powerful hallucinogenic herb.

The pleasurable meaning of Cyrus, then, is got to through accessing these transmedia narratives, across different platforms, and through different historical manifestations of her celebrity self.

Cyrus is the embodiment of the celebrity metronome. Her story begins as an idealised female teenage role model and migrates to one who is potentially toxic and wayward. Her story then has ideological dimensions: she is the subject of patriarchal law and sanctioned transgression. Her toxicity is a marketing and promotions strategy, nonetheless, to ensure career longevity and profitability; to ensure her aging fan base keep loyal, and that others will be attracted to her through the re-positioning of her brand. That she moves on, of course, allows for another Cyrus clone to emerge from the stables of Walt Disney, Inc.

2. *Transmedia storytelling reflects the economics of media consolidation or what industry observers call 'synergy'. Modern media companies are horizontally integrated – that is, they hold interests across a range of what were once distinct media industries. A media conglomerate has an incentive to spread its brand or expand its franchises across as many different media platforms as possible* (Jenkins, 2007).

The Miley Cyrus brand is intimately connected to the operations of the Walt Disney Company. As Miley/Hannah she has been marketed and sold through the four season television series, two movies, nine albums, numerous DVDs of the television series, the best-selling Hannah Montana Nintendo DS game, bedding, backpacks, toys, dolls, costumes, jewellery, make-up, and perfume. One can have a fully interactive Hanna Montana experience through the *Hannah Montana Forever* website where one can play games, accessorise, download pictures, listen to her music, watch episodes, and interact with Miley/Hannah through her laptop. One can also have *The Secret Star Makeover*, which is offered at the Downtown Disney location of the Bibbidi Bobbidi Boutique:

Girls who would like to look like their favourite pop singer have until May 1 to choose the package that includes: wig, microphone headset prop, Hannah Montana guitar purse, Hannah Montana T-shirt (size

4T-girls 16), 'Backstage Pass' makeup kit including eye shadow and lip gloss, and photo shoot with one 6×8 and four 4×6 photos and themed photo holder.

When one is asked to be made over like Cyrus, one is not just getting her look but her values and the values of commodity capitalism and the cult of what constitutes female beauty (see Chapter 2 for a further discussion of this). When one 'makes over'; as Cyrus, one aspires to be famous, to be on stage, at the media centre; one purchases beauty products and the whiff of glamour; one buys into the myth of female self-centredness.

Miley Cyrus remains connected to numerous platforms operated by the Walt Disney Company. She has released her first two solo albums and EP on Hollywood Records (owned by the Disney Media Group). She provided the voice of Penny in the Walt Disney animated film *Bolt* (Howard, 2008), for which she also earned a nomination for the Golden Globe Award for Best Original Song for her performance of the film's theme song, 'I Thought I Lost You'. Cyrus took the lead role in the coming-of-age romantic drama, *The Last Song* (Robinson, 2010), distributed by Touchstone Pictures (a subsidiary of Walt Disney Studios), and she has recently announced a fourth studio album with Hollywood Records.

3. *Most often, transmedia stories are based not on individual characters or specific plots but rather complex fictional worlds, which can sustain multiple interrelated characters and their stories. This process of world-building encourages an encyclopaedic impulse in both readers and writers* (Jenkins, 2007).

One can argue that celebrities exist in complex fictional worlds with numerous other characters and their interrelating stories. These worlds will be comprised of different settings, environments, encounters that are both public and private, with self-contained and inter-diegetic story lines that weave seamlessly together. The world of the celebrity is a fascinating fiction where we are taken from event spectacles, exotic holiday destinations, the fiction of the fiction texts they appear in (films, television shows, sports games), domestic settings, stories of home life, to scandals and expose and confessional outpourings. Friends, family, lovers, publicists, lawyers, competitors, doubters, and fellow celebrities populate these worlds, taking on various roles. Fans pour over these details, assembling their own meticulous meta-fiction of the celebrity they adore, while cultural intermediaries mine these worlds for scoops and the last word to be had on them.

Miley Cyrus exists in the fictional world of Hannah Montana, in the drama of her wayward teen years and increased media sexualisation. She exists in the private/public world of her celebrity family, headed by her mother and country singer father, Billy Ray Cyrus, who named her Destiny Hope, and in the general successes, trials and tribulations of her celebrity life.

Billy Ray is one of the central characters in the Miley Cyrus world, playing the part of her father in *Hannah Montana*, singing duets with her, and having his own celebrity image as a country singer. As she has found love, and as her behaviour has got more erratic, so his role and commentary has shifted. Billy Ray becomes the concerned father, patriarch, who chastises and comforts, and then supports his daughter. On seeing the Bong video footage he tweeted: 'Sorry guys, I had no idea. Just saw this stuff for the first time myself. Im so sad. There is much beyond my control right now'. On his daughter's June 2012 engagement to Liam Hemsworth, he tweeted: 'All I ever hoped for as a Daddy was to see my kids reach their dreams. To find happiness ... peace of mind ... and someday know ... true love'. Billy Ray, of course, is at the centre of his own celebrity universe, with a set of distinct characters playing specific roles.

4. *Extensions may serve a variety of different functions* (Jenkins, 2007).

Product and narrative extensions are the core substance of celebrity: they exist in extensive and extending universes. At a simple level, the numerous albums and two movies that were released to coincide with the *Hannah Montana* television series extended the narrative, developed characters and introduced new plot lines. The *Hannah Montana Forever* website keeps the franchise alive, and builds new linkages between fans and the show. More complexly, Miley Cyrus continues to extend the Montana universe through her own life trajectory (since they are fusion figures, as I have suggested above).

5. *Transmedia storytelling practices may expand the potential market for a property by creating different points of entry for different audience segments* (Jenkins, 2007).

Miley Cyrus's life story exists as a series of entrance points for fans and consumers to access and connect with. Her career already has two distinct phases with 'event' timelines built into her narrative. There is Cyrus as Hannah Montana; and then there is vampish and sexualised Cyrus. Connected with these stories are records, tweets, Facebook interfaces, interviews, performances, and a range of products that are sold in association with these intertextual narratives.

Access points to Cyrus multiply out and disrupt linearity. It is not just that fans and consumers have multiple entrance points to Cyrus's career, but they can access her past before her present (Hannah before vamp). They can cross-connect narrative trajectories, also, moving in and between these different access points. This will stimulate different identification streams, including nostalgia for a Cyrus that once was but is now lost (like youth itself, which will resonate with fans as they also grow older).

6. *Ideally, each individual episode must be accessible on its own terms even as it makes a unique contribution to the narrative system as a whole. Game designer Neil Young coined the term 'additive comprehension' to refer to the ways that each new texts adds a new piece of information which forces us to revise our understanding of the fiction as a whole* (Jenkins, 2007).

Celebrities are like a collection of puzzle pieces found across a large number of media. They can be understood in site specific contexts, but each new layer of their identity increases the way we can comprehend them narratively. Celebrity identification very much works on the premise of 'additive comprehension', each new text adding to our understanding of them, inflecting and transforming assumptions and presumptions previously held. Bong-smoking Cyrus transforms the way she can be read; in a sense she kills off Hannah through her transgressions. And yet the knowledge we have that she was once 'Hannah' gives added meaning to the transgression. Additive comprehension demands constant consumption of the texts the celebrity is found in and across – it fuels the engines of the celebrity industry.

7. *Because transmedia storytelling requires a high degree of coordination across the different media sectors, it has so far worked best either in independent projects where the same artist shapes the story across all of the media involved or in projects where strong collaboration (or co-creation) is encouraged across the different divisions of the same company* (Jenkins, 2007).

The celebrity is produced through co-creation, manufactured by all the sub-industries identified earlier on in this chapter. They are often aligned with the transnational operations of a synergetic media empire. They are created to be sold, and marketed across all or most of the platforms the empire is involved with. In large part, Miley Cyrus has been co-created by the Walt Disney Company.

8. *Transmedia storytelling is the ideal aesthetic form for an era of collective intelligence. Pierre Levy coined the term, collective intelligence, to refer to new social structures that enable the production and circulation of knowledge within a networked society. Participants pool information and tap each other's expertise as they work together to solve problems. Levy argues that art in an age of collective intelligence functions as a cultural attractor, drawing together like-minded individuals to form new knowledge communities* (Jenkins, 2007).

One can understand celebrity fandom as a form of collective intelligence in a mediated society. Fans pool information, share and interpret gossip, produce fanfilk and offer opinion and suggestion on the reasons for a celebrity's behaviour at any one moment. They can reveal information about ticket sales or a last minute performance, or where a celebrity might be staying. Fans can produce their own readings of celebrity texts and create fan sites where these are posted and interacted with. A knowledge community is built from this collective intelligence. There are numerous fan sites dedicated to Miley, and she has an active fan community that follows her tweets and Facebook posts. The knowledge being shared and gathered here is gossip driven, and shaped by an ideology of love, beauty, and commodity possession.

9. *A transmedia text does not simply disperse information: it provides a set of roles and goals which readers can assume as they enact aspects of the story through their everyday life. We might see this performative dimension at play with the release of action figures, which encourage children to construct their own stories about the fictional characters or costumes and role playing games which invite us to immerse ourselves in the world of the fiction* (Jenkins, 2007).

Celebrity culture is organised around active participation, the drawing of the celebrity into everyday life through play, performance, and fantasy engagements. Through various console games, one can take on the role/persona of the celebrity; through toys, dolls, make over accessories, one can write oneself into celebrity narratives; and through perfumes, dress, and jewellery one can embody the celebrity. Active participation, however, is organised around active consumption and the purchasing of play and their associated dreams.

One can buy a Miley Cyrus doll, or go online and dress your imaginary doll like Miley Cyrus, in a *Miley Cyrus Dress-up Game,* which also involves making lifestyle choices for her and helping her through everyday moral dilemmas. One can accessorise like Miley Cyrus, or wear her Hannah Montana perfume. One can get advice and information on her tattoos, her latest haircut, and how to dress like her. The immersion into the Miley Cyrus universe involves moral choices, gendered inscription, where one performs as the character would. But this can also involve subversive choices, recasting Miley through one's own point of view.

10. *The encyclopaedic ambitions of transmedia texts often results in what might be seen as gaps or excesses in the unfolding of the story: that is, they introduce potential plots which can not be fully told or extra details which hint at more than can be revealed. Readers, thus, have a strong incentive to continue to elaborate on these story elements, working them over through their speculations, until they take on a life of their own* (Jenkins, 2007).

Celebrities are involved in narratives of excess and enigma, which invite fans to offer speculative interpretation of these spectacles, leaks, and omissions. Celebrities often suggest there is more to tell, offer singular interpretations of complex events, opening up discourses of intrigue and conspiracy. A case in point is celebrity deaths such as Monroe or Kennedy, where numerous plot lines have emerged centred on conspiracy and sanctioned murder (see Chapter 2 for a discussion of celebrity paranoia).

Cyrus exists in and through these narratives of success, particularly with regards to her recent (August 2012) haircut where she got rid of her blonde locks. Numerous fan interpretations emerged, some linking it with Britney Spears' much publicised mental breakdown, when she also cut her long, blonde hair off. Narratives of excess thus connect with other celebrity stories, filling the cultural world with stories upon stories upon stories of affect.

Manufacturing Affect

One can argue that what is being manufactured when it comes to the production of celebrity is structures of affect, ripples of feeling, centred on commodity identification and ownership. In this context, one can read the celebaesthetic subject as a 'series design' meant to be experienced in and through a number of senses and sensorial experiences that are purchased and possessed. As Nigel Thrift argues, modern capitalism has begun to

> think of commodities as 'resonating' in many sensory registers at once, increasing the commodity's stickiness ... the aim is to add in more feeling by appealing to registers of the senses formerly neglected, thus stimulating the emotions connected with things, and so generally producing more affective grip for those things – and thus more engaging artefacts that produce more commitment and so sell more ... increasingly, commodities are thought of as interfaces that can be actively engineered across a series of sensory registers in order to produce positive affective responses in consumers. (2008: 39)

Celebrities are sticky, they invite sensory appreciation at a number of levels. As exalted carnal beings, often perfected, placed in narratives of affect and excess, we are asked to imaginatively touch and caress them, and to feel their touch and caress on our skin. The carnality of the celebrity may be violent, risky, hard bodied, wayward, and these qualities are also transmitted as affects. As commodity vessels, involved in selling sensory products such as cologne, or oils and skin creams, celebrities are to be smelt, touched, and one's senses and sensorial appreciation can be transformed by them (their products). Celebrities confess and emote, are affective entities with deeply affecting effects on us. Their deaths can have traumatic consequences, producing the highest registers of feeling and loss. All these forms of affect, nonetheless, are at the call of commodity capitalism, since the investment required is always tied to their images, products, and endorsements. When we mourn the death of a celebrity we do it over records, films, songs, keepsakes, mementos, and we will invest in re-releases, re-runs etc. to feel them deeply again.

The celebrity metronome is sensorial; its structure and mechanism a mixture of the soft grain of the wood, the soft ticking of its arm, made of illuminating metal. The celebrity metronome conjures up the qualities of embodied identification; its sounds and its elements affect one deeply.

Miley Cyrus/Hannah Montana (sea breeze, bubble-gum, joy, laughter, caramel)
Miley Cyrus Can't Be Tamed (heat, velvet, enigma, desire, chocolate).

5 Everyday Celebrity

All those flowers, cards, paintings, artwork, messages, poems, beer cans, wine bottles, tears, whispers, silences, songs, memories, performances, breakdowns, fuck-ups, rage, hate, love, heroin, awards, adulation, success. O Amy why do you have to leave?

Beating Quietly, Effortlessly

Celebrity culture has become so entwined with the practices, behaviours and rituals of everyday life in much of the Western world that one can argue they exist symbiotically, interdependent on one another. We experience the world and our place in it through celebrity; each and every social, cultural, and economic encounter will have in some way being connected to famed individuals and the associated products, services, and industries they are connected with. We walk in the bright lights of celebrity culture: from auratic presenters on morning TV, to star-filled gossip magazines, from Twitter feeds to music consumption, from blockbuster films to high-end gaming, from literary novels to mass tourism, and from deified billboards to supermarket shelves, the sheen and shine of famous figures is everywhere to behold. I wash my hair in the slipstream of Jennifer Aniston, exfoliate in the manner of Justin Bieber, I dress like Jay Z, listen to Adele on my iPod, and I walk out the door to a world decorated in the imagery, the discourses, of celebrity. The celebrity metronome is beating quietly, effortlessly, everyday and everywhere.

As I have outlined in Chapter 1 and throughout this book, modern life is regulated, given a regular beat, through the celebrity metronome. It provides the way time and space is to be experienced; it enchants and disenchants the world; provides the engines of ambition and desire; drives economies and the operations of transnational corporations; and critically engages us as social beings, in terms of self-worth, belonging, and success, marked in relation to our involvement with, and access to, celebrity culture. The celebrity metronome beats relentlessly if quietly, a cultural and social beat, and an interiorised beating, regulating our own behaviour in the world. The celebrity metronome is the beat of liquid capitalism, its fixed compass set in a sea of constant commodity change and transformation, where objects of desire and attraction are rolled out, rolled out, and rolled out. As Nick Couldry contends, the media is imagined to be at the centre of modern life:

> The idea that society has a centre helps naturalise the idea that we have, or need, media that 'represent' that centre; media's claims for themselves that they are society's 'frame' help naturalise the idea, underlying countless media texts, that there is a social 'centre' to be re-presented to us. (2003:46)

This cultural or ideological myth is magnetic in the way it pulls people towards this illusionary centre, a drawing towards that is psychological, physical, and behavioural. It holds us in its attraction: we think ourselves through this myth, we live in ways and through means that this myth sanctions, and we make lifestyle, career, familial, and consumption decisions based on the properties of this myth. The centre of our beings, the centre of culture and society, miraculously emerge in and through this media-narrated, naturalising myth where everyone can, should, and probably will be famous.

The 'frame' that Couldry writes of, however, has two interconnecting or sliding windows, and not one but two centres, an inner and outer. The media exists as a meta-frame on the world but behind, or perfectly fitted within this frame is the mythic, binding, naturalised material of celebrity culture. The media become the outer centre of contemporary life, celebrity the inner, very like the way television quiz shows create an elite or auratic space for those who win through to the final round. The myth of the media centre is really the myth of celebritised life, as Couldry recognises. Celebrity becomes the imagined glue that binds people together; it creates a social, cultural, and economic whole. And the media are involved in representing the representation, establishing a double-bind, an incredibly strong binding, where the world is known to have an inner and outer core through two interconnecting frames that creates and maintains the grand illusion of itself.

For example, the news media increasingly frame the meaning of poverty through the work of the celebrity ambassador. The celebrity ambassador work on our behalf, embodying the core values of ethical activity and responsive agency, and through their represented actions stand in for collective action and an organised social response. We access the meaning of poverty through the media (frame one); we act on poverty through the actions of the celebrity ambassador (frame two); and we assume therefore that there is a mythic centre we can access and should belong too, through the sliding operations of both frames that we imagine we walk into or through.

At the level of everyday life, however, we are not simply used and used up by celebrity culture but engage with it in active and affecting ways, as agents of production, as consumers who appropriate and trans-code the politics and poetics as they manifest from text to text, and from context to context. Everyday celebrity involves a series of ritualised and spontaneous interactions and creative and productive enterprises that critically complicate the mechanical beat of the metronome, the power and control orchestrated through the celebrity centre.

The pleasure one gets from everyday celebrity cannot be simply, singularly, reduced to commodity appeal. The politics on offer have radical and transgressive possibilities that counter and resist the govern-ing beat of the celebrity metronome, and the myth of the media centre. When we look at what happens at the everyday sites where the produc-tion and consumption of celebrities meet, we see affective and affecting relationships emerge.

In the rest of this chapter, I would like to employ three central case studies to examine everyday celebrity, the frames it occupies, and the affecting and challenging forces it can inspire. First, I would like to look at celebrity ritual; big, spectacular events as well as the microscopic and domestic. Celebrity ritual occupies a central time and space in the way the ordinary is wrapped up with the extraordinary. Second, I will look at celebrity in gossip magazines, particularly in relation to female readers, in terms of the productive and empowering possibilities inher-ent in gossip and the confessional mode it sanctions. The importance of emotion as a tool of radical experience, not in chime or mechanical consort with the metronome beat, will be explored. Finally, I will exam-ine do-it-yourself (DIY) celebrity and what I will refer to as celebrity citizenship, where the production of celebrity culture, and the circula-tion of celebrity happens from the bottom up, outside of, and often in critical response to, the mainstream media.

The Passion Play

Celebrity has become thoroughly ritualised in the organisation of every-day life. At the level of the spectacular ritual event, the celebrity bash, the red carpet premiere, the stadium tour, and the grand final draws one into a calendar of must-see moments where fame is at its most bejewel-led and triumphant (see Chapter 2 for a discussion of event spectacle in relation to envisioning celebrity). We incorporate these celebrity rituals into the way we schedule our daily work and life patterns, the way we organise our lives so that we can watch or attend the mega event, and through the way we make meaning of our lives through the narratives of the event, and the re-telling of those stories to friends and family. The spectacular celebrity ritual enchants the everyday, providing it with dazzle, dream, and possibility. At the same time, celebrity ritual can be argued to represent the struggles and conflicts of everyday life, if only to marginalise difference and recoup lost souls for the dominant political order, in the service of the status quo. As Kellner argues

> Such megaspectacles are part of those phenomena of media culture which embody contemporary society's basic values, serve to encul-turate individuals into its way of life, and dramatize its controversies and struggles, as well as its modes of conflict. (2003: 39)

In a heightened ideological sense, celebrity ritual draws upon the suffer-ing of everyday life through the narratives of passion so that the pain of living unequally in the world is extinguished for the duration of the event, through the body of the celebrity, and explained or justi-fied as natural and just and right. The spectacular celebrity ritual is thus a modern type of passion play. The celebrity takes on the role of the passion of Christ, they embody this type of pleasurable suffering, and we take pleasure, wrap ourselves up in the passion, which unfolds before us, and within us.

Celebrities often have wayward biographies that involve a resurrec-tion moment; their rise and fall and rise again trajectories acting act as contextual frames; and the betrayals they suffer help create a fantastic, quasi-religious ritual. Our passion rises with the rising of the celebrity ritual event, so that it takes us over, recasts our suffering, shapes a love for the celebrity which resembles, is the same quality, as our love for Christ. The suffering of the everyday becomes the passion of the celebrity ritual and we live enchanted lives, in communion with one another, in and through these spiritual encounters.

The BBC's extended coverage of the Queen's Jubilee, over a long weekend in June 2012, is an example of the celebrity megaspectacle that Douglas Kellner (2003) suggests dominates contemporary life. The coverage had all the ingredients of the heightened celebrity event, of an auratic passion play, and attempted to dazzle and enchant Her Majesty's subjects through the display of iconic objects, costumes, historic build-ings, historical events, memorials, extraordinary and ordinary people, and staged performances. This megaspectacle was supported through dramatic narrativised moments where one was asked to view or compre-hend, in awe and wonder, a spectacular happening that was taking place right before one's eyes and ears, in the depth of one's sensorium. Blink, or turn away, and something miraculous will have been missed.

On day one, in carefully edited call and response moments, the Queen, an ascribed celebrity of the highest order, gracefully waves at her subjects aboard an elaborated adorned barge as it motors along the Thames. Royal watchers on the banks ecstatically wave their Union Jacks and roar back their approval. Back at the Palace, later that day, the Red Arrows fly past in perfect synchronisation, trailing behind their engines the colours red, white, and blue. Again, one stands wide-eyed and wondrous at the British excellence before one. That night, the royalty of British pop music, Sir Paul McCartney, plays the leitmotif of *Live and Let Die* and pyrotechnics light up the night sky and the historic Buckingham Palace behind him. Once again participants roar and scream, and scream and applaud. For those watching at home, dramatic music almost magically rises up out of the television screen to cement the hyperreality that is being offered to them. The BBC, a grand celebrity institution, becomes the extraordinary carrier of such sublime enchantments. Passion is everywhere, discord vanquished, and harmony rules the waves.

This is celebritised Rule Britannia, in image and display and grand gesture, and in the thin sheen of lost objects and Empires, if nothing else of substance. All of Britain's sons and daughters are asked to take part to mythologise the inclusive nature of British society and to suggest the Queen is adored in all her former colonies – Oz Kylie (dressed as a pearly queen) and Oz Rolf Harris (full of servitude), two heightened embodiments of this internationalist celebrity appeal.

Because this *is* also an international or global spectacle. Tourist Britain is being marketed on the myth of heritage and royalty and home-grown celebrity, cosy pubs, misty moors, thatched cottages, Crown Jewels, beefeaters, ancient castles, and quality broadcasting, so this long week-end becomes essentially an extended advert to come to Cool Britannia. Let it rain, as it did for a while, Britain cannot be defeated in its spec-tacular reincarnation of the branded, celebritised nation-state.

At the centre of the spectacle is the spectacle of the BBC, Auntie Beeb, a glittering broadcasting institution, personified as a royal family member. BBC cameras are positioned at all the central points, high, low, and in amongst the crowd, while its reporters and commentators, both on the ground and in the studio, provide one with the heightened language, the higher order abstractions, that turn Great Britain into a wondrous utopia.

Lavish metaphors greet the weekend's proceedings. Clothes, settings, and crowd behaviour are turned into hysterical exaggerations. Here in this wonderland there is no recession, no austerity, no one is out of work, or is struggling to pay their bills; there is no social division but only unification and togetherness. Here there is only passion.

We are asked to suspend our disbelief and to forget that the symbolic centre of the nation no longer exists except at the myth of a celebritised media core. The re-constituted nation re-imagines its present and everything – for a while – is glorious. The television, the box that used to sit in the corner of the room is again ghosted into symbolic view, as families are imagined to gather round it to reconnect past and present, to resurrect the traditional British family that is no more. The sale of roast beef was reported to hit the roof during the celebrations, as if eating the passion of the country would make it strong and confirm one's allegiance to the Crown.

The BBC is the only organisation that can offer us such a diabolically loaded hand: it exists at the fabric, the mythic centre, of the British media, so only it (*she*, this grand old Aunty, this achieved/ ascribed celebrity) can ask us to return to the domestic setting, to be one together again, for this long, long, weekend. For this long weekend, from Land's End to the John o' Groats, British people are seen to unite behind the spectacle of the imagined nation-state.

This is a type of passion play, there is redemption for non-believers and doubters (anti-royals) if only they get with the programme; and there is a resurrection for the Royals, fading celebrities, has-been singers, second-rate commentators, as they are simultaneously and collectively bathed in this enchanted light. Their suffering becomes our collective passion. The trauma of the recession, of social division, of privilege and class are miraculously healed, or so it seems. Everyone can have cake. However, like all plays, like all celebrity rituals, the drama has to end, and not everyone signs up to be ritual members.

The BBC came in for some sharp criticism for its coverage of the Jubilee, with over 2,000 complaints received. Stephen Fry tweeted that the four-and-a-half hour Thames River Pageant was 'mind-numbingly tedious. This is eggier and cheesier than a collapsed soufflé. Expected better of the Beeb'. Newspaper columnists such as Gillian Reynold for the *Daily Telegraph* thought that coverage of, and commentary on, the

River Pageant was inane, with nothing of substance to hold the beauty of the images together.

One can argue that this was a failure of ritual – a crack or leak in its ideological centre – that people were able to see through its emptiness and quickly became bored and critical. One can thus read the (celebrity) ritual as inherently anti-structural, creating a new type of time and space that allows for, perhaps demands, a different type of self-reflection and critical awareness. Through the experience of heightened ritual one sees that the everyday world, as it exists outside of this enchanted time and space, is lacking, or wanting:

> Through the performance of symbolic stories that represent anti-structures, rituals interrupt and generalize the existing space and time in which participants live, temporarily transposing them into a different, alternative spatial and temporal system. The anti-structure of liminality allows participants for a short time to see themselves and the world around them differently, even though at the end of the story they end up reintegrating the difference within the dominant ideology. (Csaszi, 2010:2)

One could alternatively argue, however, that the pageant wasn't spectacular enough – that it didn't have the wonderland aesthetic of the pop festival that followed that night. Rather than an ideological leak, then, it demonstrated how encultured people are into the logic of the megaspectacle. They wanted more, they wanted bread and roses. They wanted celebrity passion.

The day after the Jubilee celebration, *The Guardian* reported that unemployed people had been hired as unpaid stewards to line the streets and banks where people would be gathered to celebrate the festivities. A number were assigned to steward the River Pageant that was considered such a dud in terms of the BBC's coverage. This marked a dramatic punctuation point in the coverage of the event and brought one starkly back to the reality of modern Britain in the age of austerity. After this long, long weekend Britain returned to its harsh truth, a nation divided, living off its past, haunted by its present, struggling even to manufacture a passion play that would hold the nation together. In these liquid modern times, the centre cannot hold together for very long and the BBC is just a brand. What it needs then to sustain itself is the next spectacle in the megaspectacle event calendar... this weekend the soccer... then Wimbledon... then the Olympics ... bread and roses, bread and roses, bread and celebrity.

The Shine of Shrines

As a culture we have incorporated celebrity into everyday rituals, occasions, and behaviours. Our diaries will have the birthdays of famous people we are interested in, pencilled in. We celebrate their birthdays as we do a close friend or family member; cards and presents are sent. We will follow and respond to their tweets, Facebook postings, so that their conversations are our shared conversations. On a daily basis, we produce gossip from these exchanges. We will schedule aspects of our lives to see their latest film, television show, video release, and media performance. It is felt that these must-see moments cannot be missed. Celebrities are fantasised about in diary entries and in letter, email, and social media postings. Celebrities are collected and memorialised in personal photographs, taken at gigs, events, and chance meetings. They become part of the narrative of life journeying, of growing up, getting married, nostalgic re-visitations; they are the glue of major life events.

As teenagers our bedrooms become shrines to the celebrity: walls are devoted to their pictures; parts of the room are given over to their images and products, and are touched, embraced, cuddled; and the design of the bedroom maybe an exact replica of the one our favourite celebrity sleeps in. One part of the bedroom may actually be a shrine to a (dead) celebrity, with a holy table dedicated to their memory.

The shrine may be prayed to, tended to with love and care, and at key anniversary moments will take on extra significance as that time is marked as heightened, requiring a ceremony (Wang, 2007). Wishes may be called for in front of its alter. One can be instructed on 'how to build a shrine to your celebrity' at wikiHow. Shrines can be called sacred, such as is the case, with the *Shrine of Jon Bon Jovi Reliquary* in New Orleans. Bedroom shrines are solitary; they belong to the keeper, but connect fan to fan in emotional communication exchanges where group belonging and identification takes place along a symbolic corridor from one house to another.

Shrines are also public, collective, and emerge 'spontaneously' after the death of a celebrity. *Celebrity mourning* becomes an embodied, timely, and spatial response to what is seen and felt as a personal and collective loss, as something that tares a whole in everyday life. When a fan hears about the death of a loved one there are a series of stages they go through, although these would not necessarily be uniform and linear.

First, the fan responds with disbelief and denial when they first hear about the death of a celebrity they are emotionally attached to: *it isn't true; is it true?* These questions, and the questioning of facts, will be done through personal and media communication channels – tweets and updates will be viewed, friends will be texted and called.

Second, there will be acceptance and grief involving an embodied response; the fan cries, weeps, convulses or is left momentarily paralysed, in a state of shock. Again, these will be private and public outpourings, centred on a shared familiar location where friends will gather to cry, or they will journey to the site where the celebrity met their death – where the news media will be at hand to capture what they will then represent as this ritual of hysteria.

Third, there will be demonstrations of loss and affection. These will include holding up photos of the celebrity, wearing their signature clothing, and creating a shrine of remembrance at the location of termination. These shrines will then become anniversaries and memorial.

Fourth, the television, print, and magazine industries will cover the death in a ritualistic way, commenting on and adding to the sense of personal and collective loss. They become agents of this ritual of hysteria.

Finally, various media industries will be involved in the re-packaging and promotion of the celebrity through re-releases, re-issues, special editions, and the like; and fans will consume these products to keep the memory of the dead celebrity alive.

When Amy Winehouse died in July 2011, two shrines appeared outside her North London home: the first, a shrine of bouquets and soft toys, and goodbye cards; and the second, a shrine of beer cans, wine bottles and glasses, and cigarettes. Over 200 fans gathered around the co-located shrines. *The Mail online* reported

> Remembering Amy: A shrine of gifts, flowers, cards and artwork as well as beer cans and vodka bottles have been left outside Amy's house by mourning fans … Skinheads, goths, drunks, businessmen, grandmas, young mothers, dreadlocked youths, a girl with lime green hair. All were Amy Winehouse's audience – and yesterday all were part of the show.

The Guardian reported on the messages left, including, '"Dear Amy Winehouse", read the card written in a child's handwriting, and attached to the fluffy rabbit. "Your music was the best"'. And in interview with Olivia, 22, a neighbour, they report

> People were sitting around on the pavement like at the end of a house party when something's gone horribly wrong … Today, it's

much more peaceful ... It's a love-in, really. As if they're waiting for her to come out alive.

The two reports suggest a collective communion across all social classes, ages, subcultures, and professional groups, as if Amy's death has affected everyone, and her loss is shared by all. Both, but in different ways, suggest a resurrection; her memory, her genius as an artist will live on, and it will become the main story rather than the one of her battling booze and drugs. The memorials to her confirm her standing, her religiosity, as does the sense that she may again walk out of her front door at any moment.

The ritual of grieving for a dead celebrity may be cathartic, a mechanism to deal with death; it may ultimately work to support social cohesion. However, one may also see celebrity mourning as anti-structural, grieving as a carnal response to loss, as a response to liminal experiences, which open up mourners to doubt and confusion, rather than closure and cohesion. This is can be seen as ritual of philosophical questioning and phenomenological experience.

With regards to Amy Winehouse, for example, she embodied a particularly transgressive and aggressive form of female agency, empowerment, and yet she was also a conduit of/for suffering and misery in the face of betrayal and conformity. When she sang of, 'I cannot play myself again, I should be my own best friend; Not fuck myself in the head with stupid men', she draws attention to gender as performance, and romantic love as wasted on pathetic masculinity. Her passion, then, was one of chaos and dissolution as resistant to order and unity. Her confessional song lyrics, and her confessing public appearances, are the discourses out of which opposition and refusal grow; they are sensed, and they become embodied. One can argue that celebrity gossip also works as a ritual of refusal to patriarchal norms.

Talking Up

On the front cover of *OK!* 3 September 2012 edition, the headlines tell us that 'Jessica heartbroken', and that 'her family destroyed'. Jessica (her surname, Simpson, is not used in the cover story) is photographed looking tired, with her husband's arms around her, while in an inset, positioned to the side of her face, she is pictured on one side of her father, with her mother taking the other side. Underneath the headlines we learn, in bullet point grammar, that:

- Jess' parents are heading for divorce
- Inside her father's prison nightmare
- Too stressed to diet – her desperate plan to get thin

The cover story offers us the form and content of celebrity gossip, and begins to situate the reader within a heightened family melodrama or soap opera. The exaggerated headlines are written as if they are to be spoken or whispered, as if the person who is the subject of the gossip is not physically there. Jessica's image thus becomes the relay of memory and predictive imagining, what the gossiper's would see or recall (in mind's eye) when outing her. There is revelation and surprise, and a clear sense the story will continue. One is meant to read the cover story and share it with friends, gossip about it. Jessica's image then becomes evidential, proof she is close to the edge. *Look* at these pictures, *see* what it confirms; Jess is on the slide.

The cover story touches upon two of the cornerstones of domestic, gendered or female gossip: family breakdown and personal crisis. Jessica seemingly faces three trials and tribulations: the divorce of her parents, her father's possible incarceration, and her personal battle against weight. There is a crisis in reproduction being played out on this front cover, as there is with much of celebrity gossip. The traditional family unit is breaking down, fathers are being absented, and the struggle for control of the woman's body is being explored. Jess has only recently given birth and here it is reported (gossiped) that she is struggling with her weight, and the simultaneous demise of her extended family unit.

This sense that the *OK!* cover produces and promotes gossip is supported by the minor stories: 'Jen's wedding planner reveals all'; and 'Kanye begs Kim: don't turn me into your mum'. There is no need for surnames on this cover page of *OK!* It is not just that these figures are so famous that they don't need to be written, but that they are imagined to be part of friendship circles and close/closed gossip communities. We are all on first name terms is the implicit call of the magazine. And it calls on us to gossip, to talk up, there is 'an incitement to discourse' (Foucault, 1990: 17) about our celebrities.

According to Foster (2004), gossip fulfils four important social functions. First, gossip is about information flow and exchange; it is a type of individual and collective mapping of the social world outside of its central lines of communication. Second, gossip is seen to be a form of pleasurable entertainment, involving the joy and frenzy of gossiping with one another, in spaces not public, in conversations where someone is being omitted. Third, gossip is about friendship between people and the intimacy that generates from revelation and disclosure – gossip as community building and the creation of a sense of closeness. Fourth, gossip involves the power of influence, the shaping of opinion, or changing the behaviour of the 'sinner'.

With regards to celebrity gossip there are necessary inflections or diversions. First, celebrity gossip is a central part of the mainstream media communication flow: it is in effect gossip that is being sanctioned and openly trafficked. Second, given the gossip is on an individual who is only known through mediation, supposedly through para-social connections, the level of pleasure may be heightened because there are less real-life consequences and one can increase the range and frequency and 'bite' of the whispers. As Turner suggests, paraphrasing Gamson, 'celebrity gossip is a much freer realm, much more game-like than acquaintance gossip: there are no repercussions and there is no accountability' (1994: 176). Third, any sense of influence is deferred or rendered second-hand: gossipers 'speak' only after the opinion has been set by the media frame. Julia A. Wilson contends that this gossip frame is a post-feminist, neo-liberal one which helps produce a new type of gendered body. Celebrity gossip magazines

> [i]nvites a new form of star gazing that might be more accurately described as star testing. No longer simply a key component of the star-making apparatus or a valuable cultural resource for subordinated groups, contemporary celebrity gossip targeted at 'younger and hipper' female audiences functions more as a mainstream cultural testing center for the development of appropriate gendered selves. (2010: 30)

Wilson sees this gendered development as comprised of a combination of 'self-evaluation and testing' (ibid.). The reader of celebrity gossip measures themselves against the actions, behaviours, and consumption patterns of their stars, and they test them against standards of emulation and lifestyle. In a sense, female readers become governed by this process – their own self-worth and agency bound up with the gendered talk of the celebrity. This has the potential to re-inscribe gender roles, to create a post-feminist discourse that marries fashion and mothering, consumption and domesticity, and a body that has to be beautiful and domestic, that goes to work and is reproductive. To return to the opening case study of this section, this is the governance that is being wrapped around Jessica Simpson – this is the test that readers will make in relation to her reproductive crisis, a crisis born of the body, fashioned in consumption, a life that is lived in gendered self-evaluation.

Joke Hermes has of course taken a radically different position with regards to celebrity gossip. Hermes sees reading celebrity gossip as a serious business that revolves 'around fantasies of belonging: to an extended family or a moral community' (1995: 132). Female readers feel like they are bringing a celebrity into their everyday world, both filling it with the extraordinary, while making them ordinary. The dramas, the heightened or excessive failings, and the questioning of morality that gossip involves, gives enunciative power to the gossipers. Celebrity gossip gives female readers equitable access to the media centre, which they use for collective bonding and feminine/feminist interpretation.

Rebecca Feasey suggests that celebrity trivia is a 'form of knowl-edge that awards them respect, status, and a privileged position among their peers while using these self-same discourses to connect with other women, far removed from any sense of social hierar-chy' (2008: 690). Similarly, Joshua Gamson sees celebrity gossip as involving an audience who reject the vertical (up/down) relation-ship between celebrity and consumer for a horizontal one involving a collective or shared evaluation, implicitly critical of the celebrity system (Gamson, 1994: 177–178). A collective and empowering voice emerges through celebrity gossip that renders gossip a politi-cal, liberating tool of identification, and progressive social cohesion. Hermes also suggests that celebrity gossip involves a melodramatic function:

> The repertoire of melodrama can be recognised in references to misery, drama and by its sentimentalism and sensationalism, but also by its moral undertone. Life in the repertoire of melodrama becomes grotesquely magnified. In the vale of tears that it is, celebri-ties play crucial and highly stereotyped roles, reminiscent of folk and oral culture. (Hermes, 1995: 80)

The deployment of melodrama to understand celebrity gossip can be extended to the celebrity confession or the moments where revelation comes from the mouth and body of the celebrity. This is where the celebrity takes on the gossip shared about them, and attempts to take charge of the revelation streams, opening up themselves to a sensorial exchange that openly resists their governance and control.

The celebrity confession is often melodramatic in form; the revelation tearful, there is nervousness, heartfelt honesty to the outpouring. The confession is set in a space that is meant to aestheticize the encounter, sensationalise the outpouring. This may be a darkened television studio, in the celebrity's front room, or in an 'accidental' public place that is rendered extraordinary by the very fact the celebrity has broken down in some way.

Viewers or readers readily meet the celebrity confession with a bodily response: they emit the same signs, are caught in the grip of their own bodies confessing a shared pain. While the confessional can be read as manufactured, a public relations exercise to stop or assuage the flow of damaging gossip, it can also be read as a carnal moment that works against the constructed and the representational. The melodramatic excess cannot be easily or simply recouped in the service of the media industries or patriarchal ideology. Celebrity and reader feel a shared pain; experience an embodied, cross-modal coming together. This is best expressed as a celebaesthetic confessional encounter.

When it is a damaged female celebrity, caught in the grip of a damaging patriarchal lifeworld, confessing to female fans about their woes, an experiential doorway opens up between them involving a realisation and a sensorialisation of hitherto unseen (if not unfelt) governance. I have argued elsewhere (2011) one can read Britney Spear's head-shaving act as a type of revelatory confession where she is not only rejecting her sexualised and erotic celebrity image, but also removing herself from reproductive femininity and motherhood. Britney's long, flowing, blonde hair is employed to confirm her idealised female beauty and to be a visible symbol of her reproductive power. Britney's skinhead rejects her own idealization and denies the womanly body that is meant to be fertile.

The female celebrity confession, then, not only draws attention to a/their crisis in relation to reproduction, and to their own manufactured and damaging celebrity image, but also transmits their pain through bodily affect. Their carnal body refuses governance, senses its own unease, leaks a truth that cannot be spoken and which cannot be undone. This is a positive type of celebrity citizenship involving self-determination and active agency.

Make Me Over

One can define celebrity citizenship in two opposing ways, each with different media or technological and cultural origins, and effects or consequences. On the one hand, celebrity citizenship can be argued to involve the creation and maintenance of good citizenship through celebrity identification, and the incorporation of celebrity values, behaviours and lifestyles into everyday life. It is through the tropes of celebrity culture that one becomes a good citizen; it is how one attains citizenship.

On the other hand, celebrity citizenship can be seen to be the way to get greater access to, and have active involvement with, famed figures – a situation that has arisen through the 'democratic' openness of digital and social media. Do-it-yourself celebrity, amateur celebrity blogs and fanzines, and celebrity trolling have arguably transformed the democratic potential of celebrity culture, opening up a new dynamic agora, a public space that can actually be anti-citizen, politically radical. I would like to take each of these positions in turn.

Celebrities are very often imagined to be exemplar citizens. They are seen to work hard, and to have high ethical and moral standards. They are seen to raise their children well and pay their taxes. Their lifestyles promote the good life, a life of consumption, a reward for hard work, and in turn this relationship between hard work and success is communicated to audiences to be the essential essence that should define us as good citizens too (Redmond, 2006).

Of course, when celebrities are seen to be underserving, morally bankrupt or toxic, when there is a gross mismatch between wealth, conspicuous consumption, and activity, they draw attention to a crisis in democracy if only, ultimately, to shore it up. The failure of celebrity legitimacy in this case works to verify those who justly deserve their celebrity citizenship. Although, to turn the argument one final way, this anti-citizenship may again be played out in ways which liberate celebrities and fans from the chains of a democratic logic that is a really mask for patriarchy and power, an observation I will return to later.

Brenda Weber has very usefully analysed US make-over-themed reality shows in terms of how the process of self-transformation creates a belief that to be a model citizen, who loves and who can be loved, one needs a consumption-based lifestyle. One has access to this via a meritocratic process of celebrity-inspired emulation, as Weber concludes:

The notion that good looks, a beautiful house, or a pimped-out ride are requisite for full citizenship in a larger dating, employment, and social culture manifests consistently through all of the U.S.-based makeover shows. (2009: 45)

Weber suggests that there are six distinct stages or narrative parts to the make-over show, leading to an individual's self-transformation. First, the individual is shamed or suffers shame in some way: there is a confessional exchange, she is defined or defines herself as miserable. Her body, clothes, hair, and face are her enemy. Second, a surveillance regime begins; she is put under the microscope; her bad habits are documented and reviewed. The surveyors are family and friends, the audience of the show, and a team or panel of experts. Third, there is the surrender to the surveillance regime, agreement to change and transform: an agreement to become the swan (that is actually already within her, like a signet waiting to be transformed). Fourth, there is gradual transformation, a journey often marked by ups and downs, trials and tribulations. Fifth, there is the *spectacle of the reveal*, when a new, more confident, beautiful, happier individual emerges from behind the curtains, accompanied by a televisual aesthetic that bathes the individual in warm lights. Finally, there is euphoria, with the individual gushing about how beautiful they now really are. Family, friends, audience, and experts share in this sense of triumphant resurrection. As Weber argues, the make-over themed show is a 'quasi-religious narrative' (2009: 31) where toxic excess and waist are eradicated, and a healthy, happier you emerges into the light.

The new you is often modelled on a celebrity, or mirrors celebrity culture. Beauty is defined as being youthful; it has idealized features that come straight off of the celebrity body; it is self-confident and desirable and is assisted by clothes, make-up, jewellery – all manner of commodities endorsed by celebrities. This is a new religion of cosmetics and clothes and celebrity, a resurrection into new citizenship that endorses neo-liberal capitalism, celebrity culture, and patriarchal governance.

Trolling

The proliferation of broadcasting models in the 1990s, the development of new media narratives and genres that focus upon the ordinary and everyday, and the rise of the digital and social media over the last ten years or so, has created a sense that there is a new citizen-driven democracy in play. This democracy has been argued to grant everyday citizens equal or greater access to the media (and to democratic structures, therefore) in three main ways.

First, in terms of content, ordinary people now populate much of the output of the broadcast media. Second, in terms of production, ordinary people create much of the content, particularly in the new portals of the digital media. A great deal of this content can be argued to be overtly political, aimed at keeping a check and balance on governments and business corporations. Third, in terms of reception and consumption, ordinary people can choose what, where and how they watch or listen to a programme, determining their own schedule patterns, deciding on their own markets. John Hartley has termed this turn to the ordinary as a positive one since DIY Citizenship involves active agency, social justice, and the recasting of the self:

> DIY citizenship is a choice people can make for themselves. Further, they can change a given identity; or move into or out of a repertoire of identities. And although no one is sovereign in the sense that they can command others, there is an increasing concentration on self-determination as the foundation of citizenship. (1999: 178)

Celebrity citizenship can be argued to be a variant of this type of self-determination, in all its forms. First, ordinary people are increasingly visible and vocal in the arenas where celebrities are circulated or transmitted, and take up positions as 'ordinary' celebrities through the fame they get from appearing on reality TV shows, writing successful blogs, and notable appearances on YouTube.

Second, ordinary people produce much of the content that defines a celebrity's output that helps shape their celebrity image. Through blogs, fanzines, fanfilk, diaries, tweets, video footage, and Facebook messaging, the 'story' of the celebrity increasingly happens in and through the communication channels of fans and consumers. This content can be critical; can unpack the ideologies of the celebrity in question and the system that produced them.

Third, the media channels that celebrities can be accessed on has multiplied, and ordinary people can schedule their reception on their own terms, on mobile platforms, and on sites that are not authorised by the celebrity. The low-cost entry requirements of much of the digital media has meant access to the means of production has massively increased, facilitating content generation by fans, and facilitating interaction in quick time. As Henry Jenkins (2010) suggests

Across the 20th century subcultural deployment of emerging technologies have paved the way for a greater public expectation that they will be able to meaningfully reshape the media they consume. The rise of digital networks is facilitating new forms of 'collective intelligence' which are allowing groups of consumers to identify and pursue common interests. Alternative forms of cultural production, such as those surrounding fandom and other subcultural communities, are gaining much greater visibility as they move through emerging platforms. Skills acquired through participation in popular culture are spilling over into education, politics, and religion, reshaping the operations of other core institutions.

Nonetheless, Graeme Turner has cautioned against having such an enthusiastic approach to the idea of celebrity citizenship, preferring instead to use the term 'demotic turn' to describe the shift to ordinary people having greater access to the media, to celebrity culture. Demotic is a terms that suggests in, of and for the people, but not necessarily with a corresponding increase in power and authority. In fact, much of the material that is generated by celebrity citizenship may ultimately be in the service of media institutions, raw capitalist profit, and contribute to the continuation in power inequalities. As Turner writes

> The reason for such a cycle is the pursuit of profit by large internationalized media conglomerates who, despite the demotic turn in representation and consumption, still control the symbolic economy.
> Notwithstanding the webcam girls, the trading of music on the Internet, the availability of digital production technologies in all kinds of media forms, this is still in the same hands it has always been. It might be seductive to think of the Internet as an alternative, counter-public sphere and in many ways its chaotic contents would support such a view. But, it is still a system that is dominated by white, middle class, American men and increasingly integrated into the major corporate structures of the traditional media conglomerates. (2004: 82)

The practice of celebrity trolling seems to warrant reading from both these democratic/demotic positions. On the one hand, trolling can be seen to be a critical engagement with the celebrity; a clever, considered interjection to create debate and to question their activities and behaviours. On the other, trolling can be seen to be deliberately inflammatory, destructive, a hate-filled polemic that intends to wound, which causes pain for pain's sake. The former arguably moves democracy forward, while the latter is democratic pretence, leaning on fascistic impulses, no more than a perverted will to power. As Tim Dams suggests

> Trolls aspire to violence, to the level of trouble they can cause in an environment. They want it to kick off. They want to promote antipathetic emotions of disgust and outrage, which morbidly gives them a sense of pleasure. (2004)

Australian TV host and former Australian Next Top Model, Charlotte Dawson, was hospitalised after a Twitter attack in August 2012. Dawson had recently taken on cyber-bullying, after one of her Twitter followers had tweeted her, and another fan, who had recently lost a their partner to suicide, to 'go hang yourself'. Dawson had traced the tweet and had outed the person who had sent it. She was then subsequently targeted by social media trolls who inundated her with over 200 tweets, many of which attacked her appearance, and suggested that she should kill herself. Dawson re-tweeted such messages as 'neck yourself you filthy slut' and 'please put your face in a toaster' to share what she was being put through. Trolls also sent images of dead bodies covered in blood with messages such as 'please hang yourself promptly'.

One can see that in Dawson's hands, and the hundreds of other fans who tweeted her with support for her anti-bullying stance, that celebrity citizenship has many of the qualities of strong political behaviour. The person that Dawson outed was suspended from work; and the cause of cyber-bullying reached the national media because of it. However, one can also see how celebrity citizenship is actually an arena for hate crimes and pathological behaviour. Much of the tweets were gender encoded, focusing on body and beauty, and so trolling was fashioned in the red eye of patriarchal misogyny (even though many of the people tweeting were women).

I think, nonetheless, there may be a third way of understanding celebrity citizenship in this context, as a type of anti-citizenship and a rejection of pale democracy. The desire for violence, the expression of rage and disgust, in the hope that it will be requited, is a particularly anti-structural and carnal response. It speaks against governance, regulation, and conformity, and instead invites the carnival into the world.

While my argument here is not to forgive or excuse misogyny, race hatred, and homophobia, it recognises the repressed forces that lurk in civilised society. Celebrity culture invites this type of extreme response since celebrities are very often anti-structural and carnal agents. So, while their make-over moments might sell us commodity citizenship, their heightened existence, their carnal ways, invite the sensorial rage of identification and misrecognition, a point I will explore in the final chapter.

Amy Winehouse (fire, red wine, sleep, needles, purple bruises, heart, song, hurt, loneliness).

6 The Loneliness Room

I am at the Grace Kelly: Style Icon Exhibition at the Bendigo Art Gallery, Australia. The exhibition consists of a collection of Kelly's 'spectacular film costumes, haute couture gowns from Dior, Balenciaga, Chanel, Givenchy *and meticulously-tailored suits and American casual wear'. These clothes and accessories have been given a linear history, employed to chart Kelly's life from poor immigrant upbringing, to Hollywood star, to fairy-tale Monaco Princess. One is required to move with the crowds in a linear fashion, from one glass box to another, on pathways that have to be taken in succession. Hundreds are here today, eying every detail, marvelling at the dresses, seeing Kelly's life emerge through fabric, colour, and affecting design. Kelly emerges not as a style icon but as a fusion of sensory artefacts, living in the remnants of her past, in a strange museum in Bendigo.*

Celebrity Contagion: The Strange Museum/ Mausoleum

At the online Celebrity Possessions Museum, we learn that Katie and Michelle began their collection of objects/things once owned by celebrities at the *New Kids on the Block* concert on 15 November 2008, when Donnie Wahlberg gave them his water bottle to keep. 'Since then, they have collected possessions from celebrities at concerts and other various events they have been to. Some of the submissions are from friends of theirs that have agreed to contribute to the museum'. Katie and Michelle post

> So we look over the railing, and there's Danny Wood, just standing there! NOBODY ELSE NOTICED!!!!! I got a quick picture of him. I start SCREAMING, holding my hand out, and Donnie comes walking out!!! He looks at us, reaches his hand up to touch ours, and next thing I know he's handing us his WATER BOTTLE!! We take it from him, then the 'not very nice girls' behind us try to grab it. We both

held on for dear life, and right before we had to start digging our nails into the girls' arms, they let go. That was a fight we were NOT going to lose! HE GAVE US HIS HALF DRANK WATER BOTTLE!!!!!!!!! WooHoo! It was SO SO awesome!!!!! We will forever have Donnie's saliva and DNA! Hahaha! :)

The water bottle that takes pride of place in the Celebrity Possessions Museum is meant to signify as a holy relic, a celebrity totem, one that involved a miracle and a fight to keep. It also reanimates celebrity and fan through the sense that bodily fluids have been exchanged or received. Donnie's DNA is wrapped around the bottle through fingerprints and his lips touching its spout, while his saliva is found in the water, which now becomes this conferred holy water. Katie and Michelle believe they have possessed a little bit of Donnie; that they have a little bit of the sex of his celebrity through this divine water that he gave to them, his chosen ones.

The word possession is crucial; what is *not* being possessed is the water bottle; rather, it is the celebrity, their essence. Their enchanted or charmed life is being co-located in the watery thing that is owned, cherished, touched, and consumed. One can define this carnal and existential transference as celebrity contagion, or 'the belief that a person's immaterial qualities or "essence" can be transferred to an object through physical contact' (Newman, Diesendruck, and Bloom, 2011: 4) The material possession of a celebrity's personal item, then, captures their spirit and body, which through presence, touch, even/ especially ingestion, possesses and changes or transforms the new you who now holds it.

Of course, celebrity-centred advertising is also meant to work in this way; consumers are asked to buy into the message that the product contains the essence of the celebrity promoting it. However, the difference to these once personally owned celebrity items is that endorsed products are mass produced, are not literally touched or worn or used by the celebrity; they are not in the end rare or unique. The celebrity-endorsed product arguably does not have the same cultural capital as *real* celebrity possessions and the aura of uniqueness that comes with owning them.

Possession as a psychic force that takes one over can, of course, be harmful, and contagion has the association of being a deadly or harmful virus. Fans who stalk their favourite celebrity, or who commits acts of crime in their name, or crimes for them, report that they were *possessed* by the spirit of the celebrity; that they were suffering from an auratic demonic possession of some kind. One can be possessed by a celebrity without totems or relics being owned at all, and the possession can be destructive and psychotic, as was the case with John W. Hinckley Jr's attempt to assassinate President Ronald Reagan for the love of Jodi Foster (Wettach, 2011). These types of celebrity possessions constitute what Su Holmes and I have elsewhere called fame damage, the self-destruction that can emerge from wildly intense celebrity–fan relationships (2006, 287–293).

A powerful link between the idea of damage, the female toxic celebrity, and contagious possession can be made here. The female celebrity, if defined by the dominant media as toxic to culture, is seen to transfer her toxins to those fans that identify with her. Toxicity is defined as a combination of excessive consumption, wayward morals, illicit drug use, addictive behaviours, on the part of the female celebrity who carries it around with(in) her (see Maplesden, unpublished PhD thesis, Deakin University).

Fans who come into contact with the toxic celebrity are signified as similarly contagious, possessed; drawn into and defined by this wanton lifestyle they are seen to embody and enact. The media moral panics over teen and tween behaviour with regards to early sexualisation, excessive cosmetic and fashion consumption, alcohol and drug use, is connected to the female celebrities they identify with. Under the headline, *Are Hollywood's Bad Girls a Bad Influence on Teens?* ABC Good Morning America reports

> Lindsay Lohan has been scolded by Hollywood co-stars for partying too hard and working too little. Paris Hilton was arrested on a DUI charge in September. And, of course, Britney Spears has been leaving two kids at home to celebrate her newfound freedom.
>
> So with all that glitz and glamour to compete with, what are parents to do? (12 December 2006)

The report goes on to list drink, drug, and pregnancy statistics for teenage girls, implicitly connecting the activities of the celebrities they mention to wayward behaviour in teenage girls. Damage, toxicity, and contagion are being passed from celebrity to female fan, and back again, in a loop of implied destruction and disease.

The fact that celebrity possessions can be displayed in a museum, or have their own special exhibition devoted to them; or that a celebrity's home can become a museum (such as Gracelands) suggests a communal gathering at an auratic site. In these celebrity museums, curators construct personal narratives through linear timelines; life event moments are highlighted; and rare items are given the most space, the greatest light, in what are spaces of resurrected dreams and interactive fantasies.

Each celebrity exhibit will be given a dated title card and description, to anchor and narrate what is to be viewed. Exhibits will be gathered in discrete clusters, pathways will lead this way then that, and exhibition cases are styled for gazing through and into, with light and colour used to highlight features or their overall importance. The possessions are given an auratic temperature. They can almost be touched but not quite, since the protective case or a cordon around it will prevent direct access, while acting as a resting and viewing point. We are asked to stand in contemplative awe, wonder, and desire, before these celebrity alters which should not be breached, entered, or touched, so rare, so special, so holy are its contents.

The mechanical beat behind the organisation of the exhibition is of course the celebrity metronome, drawing the spaces and times of the celebrity's life into regulated, enchanted order, in turn regulating the desire of the fans who come to sense and worship their idols. Fans who attend are meant to have their feelings and affections confirmed by the narrated sights of the exhibition but also complimented, or added to, by a 'new light' shone onto the celebrity's personal and professional life. In this collective setting, in a notable public space, the celebrity's possessions are magnified; it is as if the whole museum or exhibition is immersed in contagion. Fans leave feeling that the essence of the celebrity has been conferred on them.

There is a sense though that death also haunts these celebrity exhibitions. Very often, the celebrity is dead, and the possessions on display invoke a strange and morbid fascination with the past, and especially with those moments, objects, photographs, and memorabilia that led to death or confirmed it. When those exhibitions are concerned with those who dealt in death, such as the Peter Sutcliffe/Yorkshire Ripper display, on show as part of the *Crime Through Time Exhibition* at Littledean Jail, a former house of correction at Cinderford, Gloucester, UK, the museum becomes a mausoleum.

Described as 'the beast' on the exhibition website, the Ripper display includes handwritten 'love letters' between Sutcliffe and fan/love interest Sandra Lester; a signed oil painting of a bleak forest setting; the radio and desk lamp from his prison bedroom; and cassettes of his favourite music, including Mozart, and the The Eurhythmics, and of comedian Tony Hancock's radio show, *Hancock's Half Hour*. These items are meant to be a 'doorway' into Sutcliffe's life in jail, to his common interests. They are in a sense meant to normalise the beast while creating the impression he was innately perverse. The space (a former jail) they are housed in is meant to transport the 'fan' there, to this place where the beast of death resided. Dark tourism is a common activity, as is the trade and traffic in celebrity murderability. In this context, love interest Sandra Lester is defined as a perverse fan, attracted to Sutcliffe because of his heinous crimes, to his warped celebrity status, to the mausoleum, where her once private fantasies are now shared.

Death though is also very much about life or 'symbolic immortality' since the exhibition gives new life to the celebrity, brings them back from the dead, so to speak. The curating of their lives, and the devotion showered on them by fans, show how their lives have been extended, immortalised. Their celebrity metronome is a resurrecting beat across time and space, space and time. Of course, people who commit serial murders are often hoping that dealing in death will bring them celebrity symbolic immortality: everlasting life through carnage. Whatever the inflection, celebrity fandom and immersive identification grows and grows and grows, like a contagion set free.

The Loneliness Room

One can define celebrity fandom as involving two, sometimes inter-relating, forms, one that is individualised and individually sanctioned; and one that takes place in fan communities, defined as 'the shared social contexts within which fan reading and creative practices occur' (Jenkins, 2006). Those celebrity fans who individualise their active participation also often share and partake in communities, involving themselves in both a 'private' form of intimacy with the celebrity, and a 'pubic' one, where the sharing of knowledge, readings, desires, and the creation of homages and transcodings of existing texts takes place. According to Henry Jenkins, fandom is a key facet of participatory culture, where

> [f]andom refers to the social structures and cultural practices created by the most passionately engaged consumers of mass media proper-ties; participatory culture refers more broadly to any kind of cultural production which starts at the grassroots level and which is open to broad participation. (2010)

The participatory culture that builds around celebrity fandom can be argued to be regenerative, effecting the production and reception of the figure, as fans creatively transcode their meaning, produce and transmit new ways of understanding the celebrity, and engage in new forms of collective interaction.

In Charles Soukup's (2006) study of online celebrity–fan sites, three reasons are found for active participation. First, the celebrity fansite is constructed to be an open dialogue with the celebrity and the fan community. The fansite exists as a dynamic space to 'speak' to the celebrity, with the fan(s) hoping they might speak back, and to fellow devotees about their fandom – their cherished moments, interpretations of new events, gossip, the remodelling of the celebrity and the revision of received wisdoms about them.

Second, the celebrity fansite is seen as very much a creative space, designed to control the representation of the celebrity, to counter the dominant, mass media frameworks they may have been engineered into. Fans mine the celebrity's biography, media work, interviews, and public appearances to create their own narratives. These bottom-up narratives are seen to influence the way the celebrity is subsequently represented, styled, and promoted. Fans have active agency in the way their favourite celebrity performs.

Third, celebrity fansites are seen as spaces where personal identification with the celebrity is communicated and shared. The fansite is confessional, intimate, imagined to be one-to-one even while taking place in a public setting. These intimate fan stories of identification, desire, and longing are individualised and yet openly shared precisely because they are endlessly deferred desires (the celebrity will probably not read them, not respond, or acknowledge them; the devotion will be, to a degree, unrequited). There is a need, therefore, of an outlet for parasocial recognition and comment, acceptance, and understanding. As John Caughie suggests

> The basis of most fan relationships is not an esthetic appreciation but a social relationship. Fans have attachments to unmet media figures that are analogous to and in many ways directly parallel to actual social relationships. (1984: 40)

The *PlanetSRK* fansite, dedicated to Indian film star Shah Rukh Khan, promises 'His world – within yours', written as if by a free-flowing hand; the personal touch of the site's curator. Like nearly all celebrity fansites, there are pages dedicated to updates, latest news, discussion forums, fanfiction, status updates (linked to Facebook and Twitter sites), and photo galleries and video links. The fansite, then, offers one the opportunity to engage with Khan's film work and public life, and with fellow fans, within a community setting. It allows fans to contextualise and shape his star image; and to confess and share personal stories of affection, desire, and self-transformation in and through the way Khan is imagined to live ideally. For example, Frenchfan posted an affectionate and intimate poem after Khan had been tweeting poems from his latest film shoot, *Jab Tak Hai Jaan* (JTHJ):

Salt and sweet, your eyes, naughty ...

Untied and fluent, your laughter, free ...

Light and bright, your hair, liberty ...

I won't forget, your memories, any,

Since there's still time, for me, to be.

There is still time, for me, to be ...

Moving away, your hand, softly ...

Going away, your shade, misty ...

Walking away, your steps, from me ...

I won't forgive, the memories, any,

Since there's still time, for me, to be.

There is still time, for me, to be ... . (http://www.planetsrk.com/community/threads/shah-rukh-requests-for-poem-attempts.26695/, accessed 20 September 2012)

The poem is a mixture of seductive metaphor, longing, with Khan the unnamed, impossible love interest that eventually walks away. That the fan imagines a space of romantic coupling, that they shared this intimate encounter, and that a future tense is envisaged where they might meet (again), is a powerful evocation of celebrity dreaming. As Paul Hollander suggests

Relating to celebrities is a fantasy relationship stimulated by the shortage of genuine, face-to-face, one-on-one relationships – a futile attempt to personalize an impersonal world. When there is a scarcity of sustaining, intimate personal relationships and a decline of closely-knit, durable communities, people seek substitutes. Celebrity worship is one of them. (2011)

Celebrity worship is arguably an extreme form of fandom, at one end of what has been defined as the Celebrity Attitude Scale comprised of three sliding degrees of identification and attraction (Maltby, Houran, Lange, Ashe, and McCutechon, 2002).

First, at one end of the scale is the entertainment-social level of attitude, where one is attracted to a favourite celebrity because of their perceived ability to entertain and be socially focused. Second, there is the intense-personal attitude where intensive and uncontrollable feelings about the celebrity begin to emerge and in so doing effect one's well-being in the world. Third, there is the borderline-pathological attitude, where the fan sees their existence only in relation to their favourite celebrity, whom they imagine feels exactly the same way. Borderline-pathological fans are often stalkers, and enact fantasies of coupling. Such fan-celebrity pathologies can be attributed to two social types or social circumstance.

First, shy, culturally disconnected people, who also see themselves as lonely, find that they struggle to achieve or maintain positive social interactions. Their loneliness presses on them to find company and companionship in and through celebrity culture. Celebrities are recuperating figures that the isolated individual can invest in, talk to, fantasise over; in exchanges where they are no longer shy, alienated, and through which they feel wanted and connected (Rubin, Perse, and Powell, 1985).

One can use the metaphor of the loneliness room to understand this phenomena: the liquid modern condition produces an exasperating sense of the world as lonely, disenchanted, with the absence of close community ties as the relentless tides of commodity renewal and transformation are forced upon everyday life. Celebrity culture provides the spectacle to constantly re-enchant the world, to suggest connectedness, and grant access to the myth of the media centre, while celebrities provide idealised versions of the individuated self to connect and bond with. Fans leave their world loneliness room to access endless shared rooms that they can move through, chat in, and reside in. These open rooms grant them a degree of self-empowerment, of a fantastical sense of fixed-ness in the world.

Second, the narcissist type resonates with celebrity culture since both are honed out of self-love and suggest the need for adoration, which is perceived to be deserved and should be met. The narcissist is made in the image of the celebrity and they see themselves as a celebrity, as very like the celebrity they most identify with (Ashe, Maltby, and McCutcheon, 2005). And because the narcissist is driven by the deep need to be loved, a love that they believe is rightfully theirs to claim, and which warrants them a privileged experience in the world, they struggle to maintain social relationships. The narcissist imagines a god-like relationship to everyday life, with ordinary people not good enough for them. Not only is the narcissist like a celebrity, but also they engage in celebrity fandom as if it involves a peer relationship; they have a fanatical view of themselves and the celebrity they latch onto.

Of course, the age of liquid modernity produces this cult of the narcissist since (self) love is also imagined to be crafted out of commodities that are to be purchased. The narcissist makes themselves over through cosmetic, leisure, and fashion purchases, much in the same way that a celebrity does. The constant renewal of the self renders love a thing, with a quality that can be both deep and shallow, everlasting and ephemeral; yours to possess and in the possession of others who love just like you. Celebrity love is ultimately disposable and yet its intensity, when felt, is immense (Redmond, 2010). But what of love, and of love when it becomes erotomania?

Love and Erotomania

In reviewing and classifying memorial fan letters from women asked to reflect on their relationship to female film stars of the 1940s, Jackie Stacey finds a type of spectatorship that is constituted out of religious love and devotion. In summarising their responses, Stacey argues

> These statements represent the star as something different and unat-tainable. Religious signifiers here indicate the special meaning and status of the stars, as well as suggesting the intensity of the devotion felt by the spectator. They also reinforce the 'otherness' of the stars that are not considered part of the mortal world...Worship of stars as goddesses involves a denial of self found in some forms of religious devotion. The spectator is only present in these quotes as a worship-per, or through her adoration of the star. (1994: 143)

Celebrity love is here constituted as a supernatural force conferred on a venerated individual, not thought or felt to be of this world. As a fan, one loses one's sense of self in the heady mixture of perfected beauty, glamour, and sexuality that the film stars is imagined to be. This enchanted reverie is particularly sensorial, felt in one's body, a 'homoerotic bonding' that is not subjection before the figure but potential transgression of normative desire. Love is transformative and potentially liberating in these memorial letters of devotion.

But celebrity love can also be pathological. The mental illness erotomania involves the delusion that the celebrity a fan has fixated on, loves them in return. An imagined manifest destiny narrative is played out, which results in stalking behaviour to make true the relationship that is destined to be. The erotomanic believes that the celebrity has given them a secret signal, that they have revealed their admiration for them through a song lyric, interview, or film and television role. This erotomanic episode results in the 'return' of the affection through letter writing, texts, gifts, phone calls, and house visits. The more the celebrity declines the offerings the more the erotomanic believes it is a concealment device in the glare of the media. The fuel of pathological love is constantly ignited and the celebrity is hounded into existential crisis. Two examples play this point out well.

First, South Korean Sasaeng or 'private life' K-Pop fans dedicate themselves to following their fans at every step of their lives. Sasaeng fans are usually females aged 13–21, going first through puberty, and then through progression into adulthood. Their devotion to K-Pop stars involve serial stalking, technical surveillance and snooping, and attendance at all public events. Their desire is to be noticed by the star, to have interactions with them, in the hope of love being requited, and to share with other Sasaeng fans their tactics and successes. For example, it was reported in July 2012 that, 'Sasaeng fans install CCTV in the parking lot of Park Yoochun's home'. Park Yoochun is a member of Korean boy-band JYC, who has been the main object of Sasaeng's eroticmanic impulses.

The Sasaeng fan exists in a dual realm of interactions: on the one hand, they communicate in and through blogs and forums which are secret and secretive, and they desire more than anything to get to know the secret (private) life of the K-Pop star they stalk. On the other hand, their acts are self-publicised, their reported devotion a badge of honour; and their appearance in the media confirmation of their selfless love. Their interactions mirror the dual way that a celebrity experiences their fame; set in both private and public realms, existing in tension with one another.

However, there is also a masochistic relationship being fostered here. The Sasaeng fan allows their K-Pop idols to dominate and abuse them. K-Pop stars engage with fans in aggressive and violent ways. In March 2012, the Korean news outlet, *Dispatch*, released audio footage of JYC band members, Yoochun, Jaejoong, and Junsu, which shows the three abusing and acting violently towards Sasaeng fans. Yoochun can be heard swearing at a fan over the phone, while Jaejoong can be heard repeatedly hitting one of the female Sasaeng fans. This doesn't break the devotion of the fan to the star but seems to reinforce it, and the patriarchal power inherent in much of Korean culture.

Second, stalker, Robert Dewey Hoskins, imagined that he had a relationship with Madonna, leaving a scrawled over religious tract, named Defiled, in her call box at her Los Angeles home in April 1995. One side of the tract read, 'I love you. Will you be my wife for keeps. Robert Dewey Hoskins'. The other side read, 'I'm very sorry. Meet me somewhair (sic). Love for keeps. Robert Dewey Hoskins'. Also, on that page was a drawn circle with the words, 'be mind (sic) and I'll be yours'. Beneath this love note was the printed part of the religious tract which described how sinners who have sex outside of marriage should be killed, and those who are not decently dressed should be punished.

After initially leaving, Hoskins returned to Madonna's home to be confronted by her bodyguard, Basil Stephens. Hoskins threatened to kill Stephens if he did not pass on his note, and told him that if he didn't marry Madonna that evening he would 'slice her throat from ear to ear'. After a brief gap in time, Hoskins returned to Madonna's home some seven weeks later, scaled the walls, and was twice shot by Stephens after he went for his gun.

While on remand awaiting trial, Hoskins wrote graffiti love messages on his prison walls, 'I Love Madonna' and 'Madonna Love Me'. Underneath his bed he scrawled 'The Madonna Stalker'. When a Sheriff's deputy asked him about the love messages, Hoskins claimed that Madonna had written them, and that when he got out of jail he was 'going to slice the lying bitch's throat from ear to ear'.

This oscillation between love-and-hate, or the co-mingling of these two concepts, is found in a great deal of celebrity–fan identification, but generally contained within disappointment and rejection narratives when a celebrity has changed direction, or re-styled themselves. Teen fans of Brittney Spears responded with dismay to her transformation into a vamp-like figure, labelling her a 'slore', an elision of slut and whore (Lowe, 2003: 124–125). Hoskin's love-and-hate dichotomy is bound up in contradictory but related impulses: a desire to have Madonna, for her to be his wife; a desire to domesticate and tame her; and a desire to destroy her if she refuses his demands and commands. The transgressive image of Madonna threatens Hoskins, and his response to it tries to destroy the very thing that reveals his own inadequacy.

The psychological effects on Madonna were severe, with a series of harrowing nightmares in which she see dreams Hoskins has got into her house. At the trial she commented that she felt:

> Sick to my stomach ... I feel incredibly disturbed that the man who has repeatedly threatened my life is sitting across from me and we have somehow made his fantasies come true (in that) I am sitting in front of him and that is what he wants. (quoted in Saunders, 1998: 40–41)

Madonna is here experiencing a profound sense of unease, danger, but one that is actually contingent on the duplicity of celebrity culture. Hoskin's desire for her attention, to be co-proximate, at all costs, is a core ingredient of the meaning and worth of celebrity as it is communicated in the world today.

Celebrities very often crave fame, attention, to have the adoration and dedication of their fans. Hoskin's pathological version of celebrity fandom necessarily grows out of fame's hold on identification and belonging in the world; out of Madonna's own play with it, and immersion in it. That is not to say that she is morally responsible for his actions, not at all, or that she deserves her pain, but rather that they are both caught up in fame's love-and-hate oscillating vistas, two sides of the same coin, two different but connected ticking points on the celebrity metronome.

Celebrity as a Metronome

According to Donna Rockwell and David C. Giles (2009), the effect of fame and fandom on the celebrity is 'experienced as a progression through four phases' (184). First, there is a period of love/hate towards the experience of being a celebrity, where the celebrity covets their new-found fame but finds it difficult being in the public eye all the time. Second, there is an addiction phase where being famous is experienced as an intoxicating fix, and the celebrity is goal-focused in terms of behaving in ways which maintains and sustains the fame they have acquired. Third, there is an acceptance phase that requires a permanent change in everyday life routines to accommodate the public and private, positive and negative demands of being famous. Finally, there is an adaptation phase, where new behaviours are developed to deal with the highs and lows of fame, to create life patterns that work for the celebrity in question. One powerful aspect that celebrities seem to face is an existential crisis in the face of the interactions that fame brings them:

> From an initial desire to become successful, the celebrity experiences personal confusion and a loss of ownership of life in a depersonalizing 'entitization' process, in which participants reported feeling like a thing rather than a person of unique character ... The public wants a piece of them, to touch them, to get an autograph, to have their picture taken with the star. All the while hearing one's name screamed out, the famous person feels as if he or she is not even there. (Rockwell and Giles, 2009: 185)

However, rather than these being four temporal phases, happening in order, I would like to suggest that they are actually multi-temporal phases of return, overlap and re-birth, and that they are also simultaneously spatial phases.

The celebrity may experience hate before love in the face of their new-found celebrity status, as was the case arguably with Kurt Cobain; they may develop or are taught coping strategies before they are famous (as is the case with 'manufactured' bands such as *One Direction*); and changes in celebrity status may produce a return to love (if the change is a rise in status) and hate (if there is a decline), and which would trigger another dose of addiction, and which would require a new forms of adaptation. Adaptation techniques may succeed for a time, then fail, returning the celebrity to a period of hating who they are. The different stages may overlap or occur in anti-linear ways. A day in the life of a celebrity may draw them through all four phases.

The modern electronic media present and re-present the different phases that a celebrity may have gone through, through the way digital data, mobile platforms, and cloud servers hold these moments in time in parallel and multi-temporal streams. That is, any sense of linearity is compromised by a media that can and does present the past, present, and future of the celebrity in simultaneous communication fields. To return to the example of Miley Cyrus, we can and do access all the points of her success, from Disney child star to pop vamp, since they exist in texts and contexts simultaneously displayed and relayed. That is not to say, the modernity of Cyrus, what is happening to her right now, doesn't dominate, but it is always co-present with all the other versions of Cyrus stored and relayed at the same time. Cyrus has access to all these compass and event points, sees herself as a multiple and multiplied celebrity, not linear but a composite version, a subject made up of bits of herself. This multiplicity suggests a new type of celebrity subject, a human collage always in flux.

The spaces of engagement are also important to the temporal logic of how celebrities experience fame. There are the physical spaces of engagement, through public events and private encounters. There are the virtual and social spaces, and interaction and connection through the sites of the new media. There are the textual encounters, or performances, and the way these are received by fans, the public, and reviewed by critics and mass media intermediaries. There are the uneven spaces of engagement produced by the global flow of representations; a celebrity being received differently in different parts of the world, with different fan bases, that have their own local temporal logic. A celebrity may face an increase in fame in one part of the world while suffering a fall in another, and if that decline happens at home, in their domestic market, they may feel this loss, this symbolic death in a different way than if it occurred 'overseas'.

The celebrity has their own metronome beat, a movement that connects the phases, moves them this way then that, with its rhythm increasing and decreasing depending on context, but all moments always in play, in movement, swinging backwards and forwards, creating a crisis in (their time), an eternal present shaped in the past, already shaping the future to be made. If one was to take the career trajectory of Mickey Rourke one can see a temporal crisis in his celebrity status.

On first reading, however, one can see the sort of four phase trajectory defining Rourke's experience of celebrity. Touted as being the next Robert de Niro, Rourke experienced a meteoric rise as an actor and screen idol. Self-grandeur, questionable politics, alleged misogyny, and poor film choices dented his progression as a renowned Method actor and a formidable Hollywood star. Rourke then turned against fame and film acting, said they were fake, took up amateur boxing, had a car crash, underwent botched cosmetic surgery, and saw his film roles dry up. It was his appearance in *The Wrestler* (Aronofsky, 2008) as Randy 'The Ram' Robinson that fully resurrected his career, winning him the 2009 Golden Globe award, and BAFTA award, for best actor, alongside an Oscar nomination.

The Wrestler can be read as a metaphor for Rourke's own career, and that Rourke/Randy experience the same sort of experiential celebrity trajectory. Aronofsky has noted that Rourke was explicitly chosen for the part because of his close resemblance to the character, because his own life mirrored the storyline of the film.

Summarised briefly, Rourke/Randy is a has been professional wrestler who had achieved celebrity status in the 1980s. Making ends meet by wrestling at weekends in back street promotions, and working at a supermarket weekdays, he agrees to a 20th anniversary rematch against his most notable opponent, 'The Ayatollah' (played by Ernest Miller). This rematch involves Rourke intensifying his training regime and overcoming various obstacles. Rourke/Randy takes steroids to add muscle to his physique, and he subsequently suffers a heart attack that requires a bypass operation. He carries on against the odds, against his doctor's advice. Complicating subplots include his desire to reunite with his estranged daughter, and a hopeful romance with a club stripper, who Rourke tells near the end of the film that he belongs in the ring where his fans adore him. The anniversary wrestling match at the end of the film has Rourke/Randy clearly struggling with heart pain, climbing on to the top rope of the ring to land his signature wrestling move, a diving head butt called the 'Ram Jam'. In tears, Rourke/Randy is seen saluting the crowd before he leaps, a metaphoric moment of victorious adulation at the exact moment that death may consume him.

The parallels to Rourke's career, and to his own sense of celebrity are obvious. Like Randy, Rourke had fame and adulation and had lost it. Rourke's drinking and womanising mirror Randy's, as does his reputation for being head strong and difficult to work with. The steroids that Randy takes to bulk up are a carnal echo of the cosmetic surgery that Rourke had to have to heal and beautify his face. The low-rent part-time jobs that Randy has mirror the acting bit parts that Rourke had began playing. The chance to come back, to regain celebrity status, to do what he loves most, to be loved again, is given to Rourke as it is to Randy.

However, this is where the parallel breaks down to be supplanted by a co-existence between the two. It is through Randy that Rourke demonstrates his skill and dedication as a Method actor. Rourke worked out, took up professional wrestling, did his own stunts, lived like a wrestler for the pre-production and production phases of the film. Rourke gets to comment on the role:

> I kept getting hurt. I think I had three MRIs in two months because I wasn't landing right. These guys take several years to learn how to land and I think after I started getting hurt doing it, I started to realize these guys are really suffering and I kind of gained a respect for their sport. (2008, Entertainment News)

It is through Randy that Rourke will regain his celebrity status, the adoration of fans and critics, who can again admire his acting skill. While Randy dies at the end of the film, Rourke lives on, his success in the role secured through acting awards and further major film roles.

The sense of a linear temporal path, of a distinct four phases to experiential celebrity in this film, is undermined by the fact that Rourke fans already have access to and knowledge of all four phases of his career when they start watching the film. These phases cannot be separated; they exist simultaneously; rise up in the performance, the representation, in ways that cannot be so easily temporarily aligned. Rourke works in the film precisely because of the time crisis he embodies: the collapse in temporal logic as his past, present, and future collide and conjoin.

Rourke has a massive fan base; the sense that he needs the oxygen of fame, love, to exist, and that fans need celebrities to experience the world in an enchanted way, can be explored in one final idea, that of the celebrity carnival.

The Celebrity Carnival

One can argue that the way celebrities can experience fame, and the way fans can engage with celebrities, is carnivalesque in form and feeling. The celebrity carnival is one that stands in opposition to social hierarchy, cultural constraints on the body, routine and routinised life, and which can offer a version of the 'world upside-down'. According to Bakhtin

> In fact, carnival does not know footlights, in the sense that it does not acknowledge any distinction between actors and spectators ... Carnival is not a spectacle seen by the people; they live in it, and everyone participates because its very idea embraces all the people. While carnival lasts, there is no other life outside it. During carnival time life is subject only to its laws, that is, the laws of its own freedom. It has a universal spirit; it is a special condition of the entire world, of the world's revival and renewal, in which all take part. Such is the essence of carnival, vividly felt by all its participants. (1984: 10)

As noted earlier, the demotic term to fame (Turner, 2004) has meant that ordinary people readily and easily achieve celebrity status, and do-it-yourself celebrity is a dominant production and consumption strand in the way fame is circulated and received. As such, there is very often a collapse in celebrity role distinctions and hierarchies, even if there isn't a subsequent transference of 'democratic' power. In this respect, the social media has enabled a whole galaxy of carnival inspired sites and portals where people get to play out celebrity as if they are celebrities, free of inhibition, and where they become famous through certain performative cues.

Celebrity culture creates the impression that there is no meaningful life outside its borders, and that all who exist should take part in its reveries and dances if they are to achieve self-worth and happiness. While this 'taking part' can be argued to work in favour of liquid capitalism and its demands for commodity purchase, since the celebrity carnival rejoices in an orgy of consumption, it can also be argued to be transgressive in certain contexts and situations.

The celebrity carnival can bring into its arena the toxic, the damaged, and the rebellious, and 'fools' are readily given important roles within its heightened drama. The celebrity carnival isn't a democratic space, it isn't meant to be, but an anarchic one, involving a grotesque form of celebrity becoming, built on the logic of the chaos of the senses. Three examples bring this argument sharply into view.

First, heavy metal fans experience their favourite bands through the carnivalesque. The live gig is the perfect embodiment of this since band and fans employ their bodies in ecstatic, unruly ways. Heavy metal carnival is built on the logic of 'grotesque realism':

> Fans rage, swear, chant with middle fingers and metal horns, and other billingsgate. They body thrash, mosh, body surf, and delight in parade stripping rituals. As in Bakhtin's carnival, amid sweaty bodies pushing, grabbing, swaying, rubbing, and touching, the crowd is made 'concrete and sensual.' Among the 'pressing throng, the physical contact of bodies, … [t]he individual feels that he is an indissoluble part of the collectivity, a member of the people's mass body' (Bakhtin [1936] 1984:255). This more subtle yet powerful carnival experience may be among the most transgressive aspects of heavy metal carnival, for it grates against a society that places primacy on autonomy, self-interest, and individualism. (Hanlon, 2006: 40)

Heavy metal bands enact and embody the grotesque in similar ways, 'dramatized by a communal flow of human excretions such as spit, blood, vomit, urine, semen, and faeces' (Halnon, 2006: 36). For both performing fan and performing celebrity, the grotesque communal experience of metal music is 'dis-alienating' since it provides a space for a shared body experience that empties insides, draws back the borders, re-situates the self as an uncivil animal set free.

Second, the female toxic celebrity is herself a grotesque figure who constantly exists in a world turned upside down: she lives in and for the night, taking in an excess of sex, drinks, drugs, and alcohol. Her body is captured falling out of itself, being promiscuous, challenging sexual boundaries, stumbling, crashing, and emptying itself of vomit. She visits clubs, is seen endlessly partying, gets caught in misdemeanours, is brought before the law, which she very often refuses to acknowledge.

Lindsay Lohan may be the best example of the female celebrity grotesque: her alleged alcohol and cocaine use led to paparazzi shots of her partying, vomiting, falling out of cars with no underwear on, her vagina revealed. Lohan's nightlife adventures allegedly led to several DUI charges, probation periods, periods in jail, and stints in rehab. At one probation hearing in July 2010 Lohan had written on her finger-nails, 'FUCK U', a direct challenge to authority, to the legal system. Her relationship with DJ Samantha Ronson transgressed heterosexual norms, and allowed her to openly question sexual binaries.

In the daytime, the female toxic celebrity continues to endlessly consume but it is goods, clothes, food, high fashion, and exotic ('night filled') holidays. The toxic female celebrity refuses to work, to regulate her behaviour according to routine or routinised life, and so the carnival life continues. Paris Hilton lives this type of out-of-time toxic experience, where without talent, skill, or 'occupation', but with an abundance of wealth, she consumes and consumes to excess.

As such, the temporal and spatial conditions of a female toxic celebrity's life exists permanently in the realm of the carnival, and this is different, therefore, to Bakhtin's position that while the carnival isn't constrained by space it was limited in time, since all people had to eventually return to the ordinary world. The carnival always had to end. In celebrity culture, in this particular toxic embodiment of the celebrity carnival, there is no end to the grotesque, or to the realm of excess. The party goes on and on and on.

Female fans of the toxic celebrity can be seen to embrace the carnival grotesque experience, if media moral panics are only partly true, and if fansites and blogs tell an accurate story. Fans often live in the night in hedonistic and debauched reverie; and they consume by day. They experience their bodies in unregulated ways and find commune and communal value in doing so. Their identification with celebrities such as Amy Winehouse and Lady Gaga are built on this experience of recognising their difference and exploring it. Lady Gaga calls her fans Little Monsters, and herself Mother Monster, in recognition of their shared difference, their outsider status, their refusal to accept gender and sexual norms and behaviours, and of her role as their abject projector. Her difference, their difference, is the material out of which the carnival comes into being. As one Little Monster blogged

> Her music saved me
> You know that gaga is one hell of a person caring, talented, beautiful; this is why I love her!! Her music is inspiring and to be frank listening to her music saved me from falling into depression after being told I was nothing and belittled by people I said screw it I'm done then I heard of lady gaga she was weird and didn't care. Here is my thanks to you gaga for helping through your music it means the world to me and others out there.
> Here is my thanks to you gaga for helping through your music it means the world to me and others out there. (http://littlemonster-confessions.tumblr.com; accessed 5 September 2012)

Gaga's Little Monster is here saved from alienation by a culturally alienating force, and embraces her/their grotesque difference in a productive sense of self-worth, and outsider community belonging.

Jackie Stacey (1994) identified a series of transformatory actions and activities by fans in response to the female stars they identified with. These included 'pretending' to be like them; 'resembling' them through the choice of dress, hair, and make-up; the process of 'imitation'; and direct 'copying' techniques. These actions and activities had both psychic and physical components, involving mental-imaginary, and embodied transformations of the self. Stacey suggests that this has positive feminine and feminist outcomes, with women being able to play with their identities in self-affirming ways.

Third, satire, irony, and wit are key to the way celebrity is performed and how fans are shown to identify. The self-reflexing ways that fans make critical sense of celebrities (Gamson, 1994), and the knowing and ironic use of gossip to talk about celebrity, draws upon laughter and the power of the open mouth, to disrupt normative interactions between fans, friends, and celebrities. Laughter opens up the body to a carnal experience. Shared gossip, amongst female friends, on a weekday afternoon at somebody's suburban house, invites the grotesque back into the world, opens up a space for the bawdy, the filthy, and the scatological to take root, to uproot the domestic, to turn the world upside down.

Bakhtin (1984) argued that as the carnivalesque was forced from the world, it penetrated language and literature, which took on its sensorial qualities and drew upon the conditions of the grotesque to create the carnival experience. Much of celebrity culture is embodied in form, relies on the body to communicate its stories of love, lust, and desire. The real condition of the relation between fan and celebrity is one of/ through/in and within the body. This is the celebaesthetic relationship that I began the introduction to this book with: a relational exchange, skin-on-skin, sense loaded upon sense, that is very often primordial, carnal, and carnivalvesque. The metronome's pendulum continues to swing, and the beat is continued to be heard and felt.

I would like to end this chapter with a personal fan response, a nostalgic remembering of what David Bowie means to me.

Who Am I Now?

I am watching for the first time the video to Bowie's new single, 'Where Are We Now?', released on the day his 66th birthday (8 January 2013). Within seconds of hearing the first vibrato chords of this wistful song and of seeing the memorial images of the Berlin that Bowie did some of his finest work in, I find myself in a flood of tears. The video has acted as a 'memory text', activated a 'structure of feeling' (Kuhn, 299: 2010) that has thrown up all sorts of nostalgic impressions, affects, and ultimately takes me right back to a heightened moment of personalised time, of enchanted plentitude, as this question begins to fall from my wet lips …

Who Was I Then?

My first fully intimate, meaningful engagement with Bowie occurred when I was aged 12. I had again been in trouble at school, and had crashed on my bed, alone and lonely. It was in this mood of melancholy and introspective alienation that I put *Diamond Dogs* (RCA Records, 1974) on, while simultaneously running my fingers over the man-dog figure that spread itself over the gatefold album cover it came in. This aural-visual alignment – hearing Bowie strangely, while seeing and touching his animalised, hybrid self – allowed me to enter an enchanted world where his hybridity opened up new otherworldly spaces to exist in, and new liminal identity positions for me to 'try on' and embody (Frith, 1996; Bennett, 1999). I should note that here I am employing enchantment in the way defined by Jane Bennett, or that which

[e]ntails a state of wonder, and one of the distinctions of this state is the temporary suspension of chronological time and bodily movement. To be enchanted, then, is to participate in a momentarily immobilizing encounter; it is to be transfixed, spellbound. (2001: 5)

As I listened, my tiny room was filled with the uneven stylistic tones of the album, a mixture of the brassy chords and glam pop beats of his previous work, with the haunting, scratchy, apocalyptic tones of a future world gone terribly awry. I experienced *Diamond Dogs* as the sonic equivalent of glamorous artifice meeting the hard conditions of social realism – a musical odyssey at once familiar and strange, of, and yet also, out-of-this-world. It was as if these Orwellian[1] sounds and pronouncements spoke to the dystopian elements of my life, while its futurism lifted me upwards and outwards.

I recall now that this produced an *'unheimlich* (uncanny) feeling of being disrupted or torn out of one's default sensory-psychic-intellectual disposition' (Bennett, 2001: 5). I felt immobilised, enraptured, cut free from the physical and psychological limitations of place, space, and body, and I was exhilarated as a consequence. Bowie's music – the alien figure that created it – provided an escape from the limiting confines and regulatory conditions of my life, into a world that recognised the former while creating a space for the difference within me to be celebrated, extended, made into hopeful selfhood. Bowie's Dogs allowed me to 'experience myself in a different way' (Frith, 1996), it allowed me to create a mobile version of my self, no longer classed, materially poor, or singularly gendered but alien, polymorphous, beyond cultural signification. Bowie's music produced an alternate version of myself, as popular music regularly can (Frith, 1996).

These enchanted tracks were supported by Bowie's deployment of 'cut-up' lyrics, inspired by William S. Burroughs. This was his first attempt at cutting up complete sentences he had written, and rearranging them into lines composed of allusive juxtapositions and oppositions, drawing on literature, cinema, pulp, science fiction, and bohemian references and allusions as he did so. When Bowie sings, 'As they pulled you out of the oxygen tent, You asked for the latest party, With your silicone hump and your ten inch stump, Dressed like a priest you was Tod Brownings freak you was', one is drawn into a world of excessive consumption and bodily disintegration, the lyrics conjuring up the spirit of carnival (Bakhtin, 1984), set in a freakish marketplace. The enchanted world I experience here was far removed from the politics of my social life and allowed me to recognise myself in the outsiders who populate his songs, including, on this album (cover) his new star self, Halloween Jack, 'a real cool cat'.

Halloween Jack offered me a representation of Bowie as half man, half dog, as clearly male and yet neutered or suffering from penile and testicular agenesis. On the cover to *Diamond Dogs*, Bowie is positioned as if he is lying naked on a carnival stage, with two female-like empusae or vampiric demons either side of him – the famed creatures who folklore suggest seduce men in order to feed on their flesh and blood. Bowie's upper torso reveals the androgynous red hair and painted lipstick rock star of previous incarnations, including Ziggy Stardust and Aladdin Sane, and the lower part of the torso shows him to be a desexed dog. He is the embodiment of the text, 'the strangest living' curiosity, that runs down the side of the façade he lies underneath on this cover. I hear and see Bowie/Jack, then, in a moment of pure animal and sexual liminality. Not only do I identify with such a representation, characterisation, but also I let it take me over. I feel it (in my fingers) as a phenomenological, sensory transformation (Sobchack, 2000) where my self is hybridised, remade as animal, as dog. I am Halloween Jack, a real cool cat.

One can understand Bowie's star image at this time as being fashioned out of such border crossings. As Suzanne Rintol suggests, summarising the work of Richard Grossinger, Bowies 'sexual ambiguity and status as an alien ... provides a forum through which the collective audience might fulfill its need to renegotiate what constitutes acceptable social attitudes and behaviours' (2004). Bowie's hybridity, androgyny, alien-ness provides his fans with a space in which to border cross (Auslander, 2006).

Fans gathered around Bowie as fellow border crossers, using his star image and music as a 'badge of identity' (North and Hargreaves, 1999) to mark out, and to share with one another, their difference to those who didn't act strange, who were not part of his alien universe (Hills, 2002). In my particular case my fandom was a carnal one, made of the flesh, first properly cast in an enchanted space where I found the *sense(s)* to be someone else, someone more, a self-liberation that I subsequently took back into my everyday world, resistant and rebellious, but, the question remains,

What happened to me? And Who Am I now?

Where Are We Now is a love song to the past, drawing on images and references to Bowie's own creative period in Berlin. As he conjures up his own memorial framework, composed of lyrics that recall his time there in the late 1970s, such as, '*Sitting in the Dschungel, On Nürnberger Straße*', and shots of the places where he lived or travelled through, such as Potsdamer Platz, I am affectively positioned to do the same. The objects, curiosities, and mementos that also fill the video – mannequins, a snowflake, a crystal, empty glass bottles, a giant ear – suggest

Bowie's own memorabilia, and again ask me to draw on them to memoralise my own affective investment in his work. It takes me back to the days of *Diamond Dogs*, to the sounds, sights, smells, textures, and fabrics of my lost youth.

The melancholy of the song registers as a 'super expressive human voice' (Juslin and Västfjäll, 2008: 566) while the portentous images call on me to feel my way back into my past. As Bowie asks, where are we now?, I ask myself through an autobiographical framework, who am I now? I look back at the promise of my youth, at the hopes, aspirations, dreams I forged back then, and find the mismatches, the cracks, as well as some successes. There is an overwhelming awakening within me as I do so, a heightening of my senses, but also a deep and profound sadness as I experience my own mortality, and newly experience the span of my life as it has been lived.

There is something of a 'cruel optimism' (Berlant, 2011) at work in this encounter with Bowie's new work; while I can longingly recall the enchantment I got from *Diamond Dogs*, from man-dog Halloween Jack, the encounter with his new songs registers as a disenchantment, or rather, it has led to 'the blow of discovering that the world can no longer sustain one's organizing fantasies of the good life' (Berlant, 2012). When Bowie sings of walking the dead, I see myself in a crowd of zombies, undistinguishable from everyone else, crossing Bösebrücke, to an uncertain future. And yet Bowie and I are not yet completely used up, as the lyrics go onto suggest, we still live, we live with a remarkable fire burning within us, and I have you.

Lindsay Lohan (vodka, sweat, tears, acidic, course, lonely, free).

Note

1. A number of songs on the album had been initially written to be part of a theatrical production of George Orwell's novel, *1984*, but Bowie was denied the rights to use the material.

Epilogue: I am Celebrity

I want to be a movie star. I want to be an A-listed celebrity on the glossy front cover of OK! magazine. I want to be the subject of gossip, innuendo, and intrigue, in the blue-collar sandwich room, in the stuffy white cubicle office, and on trams, trains, and omnibuses everywhere. I want an ocean of fame to surround my name as it glows outside love-struck theatre and film shows. I want a life of excess and bohemian sex. I still want to be Kelly McGillis in Top Gun, kissing Tom Cruise. I don't want to be a scientologist though.

I want a mansion in the Hollywood hills and a cabinet of pills to cure my ills. I want a fast sports car, a private Jetstream plane, and a closet full of Armani silk suits and Gucci slippers. I want and need the applause, the spectacle of affection, and the ecstasy of personifying perfection. I want to dance with the ghost of Marilyn Monroe while possessing the body of a dead-beat, drifting juicy Jimmy Dean. Love me. Love me, please do.

I want to slow walk the red carpet, shimmer under the spot light, wave at the adoring crowd, from a sterile distance. I want be in the news. I want to be badly behaved, reckless, dangerous, angry. I want to be photographed fist fighting with the paparazzi, locked up, put in rehab, if only to rise, rise, rise, rise from the hell fall that befell me. I want to be immortal, if only symbolically so, my star name sown into history books and fanzines for now and forever.

I want to be an ambassador of fame, to help the hungry, champion the marginal, lead the protests against global warming and the cold, cold lights of liquid capitalism. I still want to be a star called Leif Memphis, an Irish dissenting, hard bodied, cigarette smoking, sex symbol of the contemporary age. I don't want to age. I don't want to get old. I don't want to die. I am celebrity. We are all celebrity. This is celebrity now.

I began the co-edited book, *Framing Celebrity: New Directions in Celebrity Culture* (Holmes and Redmond, 2006), in a similar fashion to the opening paragraph found above. It was intended as a creative way to touch upon all the core issues and processes that related to celebrity culture, as I understood it. It also functioned as a way to embody and sensorialise the acts and actions of celebrity life. The story of Leif Memphis allowed me to weave myself into the fabric, the mythology, and the phenomenology of fame. Writing the sentences were not just playful academic musings, however, but allowed me to place myself into a fantasy narrative of sights, sounds, events, and encounters. The images and their senses gave me great carnal pleasure. And pleasure has been a constant beat across the pages of this book so far.

However, there is what I would like to call the phenomena of dark pleasure that also runs though the corridors of celebrity production and consumption. These dark arts take two forms: parastardom and the cult of marginal, outsider figures; and anti-celebrity, composed of those famous individuals who detest their fame, or who lampoon celebrity, and of anti-fans, who take great pleasure in hating famous figures. I would now like to explore them in turn, before ending with a discussion of ageing and immortality.

Parastardom

Parastardom exists on the margins of cultural acceptability and visibility. While it draws from mainstream stardom, leaches off its representations and identification streams, it functions in opposition to dominant star images and their ideological and sensorial qualities. The parastar is often a transgressive and liminal figure, appears in cult texts, and is defined by their excess, both within the texts they appear in and in public life. They are excessively embodied, and their bodies are exaggerated carriers of emotion and affect. The parastar offers the fan a set of unruly pleasures, within, 'a counter-aesthetic turned sub-cultural sensibility devoted to all manner of cultural detritus' (Sconce, 1995: 372). The parastar is often trash, lowbrow, while they invite those with cultural capital to experience acts, behaviours, and sensations that canonical texts and stars cannot easily offer. They operate as border-crossings for the alienated, the marginal, and the dispossessed.

In one general sense, parastars are culturally invisible; they don't garner a great deal of mainstream media attention, unless they are thrust into the limelight for some heinous act or newsworthy event. In fact, it is their micro or sub-cultural status that helps warrant them their pariah-like status. The parastar is a paragon of bad taste and is found in bad taste sites and contexts, where one has to go looking to find them. The pleasures on offer are often based on abjection, revulsion, transgressive desire and identification, and disgust. The parastar is a grotesque figure of the contemporary celebrity carnival; they embody – to carry forward the theme from the last chapter – 'the world standing on its head' (Bakhtin, 1984: 150).

The American actor, singer, and drag queen, Divine, is a perfect example of the parastar. Although Divine died in 1988, he continues to have a large cult following who commune around his grotesque performances, particularly his film roles for director John Walters. Divine is a figure of excess, of gender transgression, occupying a male body that has enormous breasts, outlandish make-up, and died platinum blonde hair. He draws attention to the performativity of gender, engages in border-crossings, and draws upon emotional excess (witty dialogue, song, dance, melodrama, self-loathing, body horror) to connect with fans. In *Pink Flamingo* (1972), for example, which Waters defines as 'an exercise in poor taste', Divine plays Babs Johnson, 'the filthiest person alive'. The narrative of the film involves Divine proving that he or she is a filthy pervert, and the film ends with him eating fresh dog faeces off the sidewalk. Conventionally speaking, the scene is disgusting; it involves Divine actually consuming dog shit that has just been passed.

Divine takes into his body animal waste, and wipes his mouth as he does so, seemingly enjoying the taste. For viewers, this touches upon the regulation of disgust, it involves a 'gatekeeper emotion' that tries to stabilise the challenged self in time and space. However, disgust is also 'anti-democratic', unleashing forces that cannot be contained or constrained by normative ideology, by the repressive apparatus of conventional life (Miller, 2004). In being disgusting, Divine becomes a parasitic force, living off animal waste, he becomes a parastar that embodies disgust, offering viewers dark pleasures that challenge the senses, that offers them (to be) the animal within.

Anti-Celebrity

Contemporary culture is awash with anti-celebrity sentiments. As I mentioned earlier in this book, celebrity is identified as a cultural disease, that it dumbs down the news, and is seen to be involved in creating relationships that are based on false associations and which produces desires that reduce people to objects in love with shiny things. Stuart Hall's recent launch of the Kilburn Manifesto (2012) takes celebrity culture as central to the neo-liberal framework, suggesting that it is responsible for the dominance of the possessive individual, defined by individualist goals, and self-interested consumption. The mainstream media and some of its most high-profile commentators can be anti-celebrity; celebrities can be also anti (their) fame; and consumers or anti-fans can be vehemently anti-celebrity too. All the discursive threads of anti-celebrity nonetheless produce pleasure: hating itself produces identification possibilities, and hating celebrity emerges in texts and contexts that are sensorial, creative, political, philosophical, and imaginative.

Anti-fans can form in two different ways. First, through derision and distaste they can take issue against a particular celebrity for the way they embody fame, or because they compete with other celebrities they have forged close affiliations with. These celebrity haters can take their scorn into imaginative or creative work, where they write, paint, satirise, and photo-shop in self-generated art or media texts against their celebrity. A recent example of this would be the opposing fans of Miley Cyrus (Smilers) and Selena Gomez (Selenators), who threw scorn at each figure, via tweets, and Facebook encounters, and who put together YouTube videos defending one or the other. For example, in the fan video, 'Stop The Hate On Selena Gomez!! Here Are Many Reasons Why You Should Stop Noh8!' by KeshaRoCKS10, we are advised

> This is a support-video for selena gomez, she is the cutest girl ever I met fans who met her & they said she was sooo cute she always cared about them!! Thats why I love her :) I know she would never do anything bad to anyone. http://www.youtube.com/watch?v=w1y4A HKx4sA&list=PL7B767BB556F76AA4&index=1&feature=plpp_video (5 November 2012)

The video is comprised of a montage of still images of an idealised and vulnerable Gomez with overlaid text drawing attention to her virtues, and why hating her is 'pathetic'. The soundtrack over the video is Nicki Minage's *Save Me*, which has a confessional lyric that is meant to anchor Gomez's perceived pain at being hated. While the video prophesises on sharing love it draws on hateful phrases to protect Selena.

Second, anti-fans can take critical issue with the whole apparatus of celebrity culture, forming groups that openly attack what celebrities stand for. For example, the 'anti-celebrity' Twitter feed unites an active group of celebrity haters who regularly tweet on the wrongs and perils of celebrity. With over 4, 400 followers they argue: 'Celebrities are neither powerful nor beautiful. They are the political puppets of the capitalist class, distracting, numbing, and demoralizing the populace' (https://twitter.com/AntiCelebrity).

Celebrities that are anti-celebrity occupy three different camps. First, there are those whose celebrity is comprised of anti-celebrity qualities, who lampoon and satirise the(ir) celebrity self. Barry Humphries is one such celebrity whose alter-egos (Les Patterson and, in particular, Dame Edna Everage) are satires of stardom. Dame Edna embodies the gauche, the faux, and the excessive, in a parody of the chat show format and through her clamour for glamour.

Second, there are those who bemoan their fame, such as actress Kirsten Stewart, who has been reported as saying, 'I didn't like being a celebrity. It's a service job. Like washing toilets' (Vernon, 2007). These anti-celebrities position themselves as artists and celebrity is seen as an ugly veneer that spoils, gets in the way of, their craft. Celebrity is here also linked to the commercial streams of media promotion, where 'stars' are asked to promote their work in a global marketplace. There is a class and power dimension, clearly. Celebrity is low culture, is equivalent to the low end of blue-collar work, while art is rarefied and (for, by the) elite.

Third, there are those who are anti-celebrity through actively avoiding its callings and representational streams. These are not, however, parastars, but those whose work exists in minority art forms, generally outside the mass media and consumer culture more generally. Poets, ensemble musicians, authors, and installation artists would fall into this category, their minority fame built on 'antireputation', whereby they become well known for *not being* well known. These anti-stars find themselves anti-promoted through small and niche publishing houses, galleries, sittings, and local arts events that focus on their artistry, or introspection; that herald their celebrity invisibility as a sign of real, quantifiable greatness. The performance artist Orlan is one such anti-celebrity. She works in the area of carnal art, has garnered a reputation as an avant-garde artist, working on the margins of artistic practice and in opposition to celebrity culture. She is a 'star' in her own literal 'theater of operation'.

> Orlan's insistence that art is a life-or-death issue involving literal as well as metaphoric risk continues to raise the question of whether she is inspired or crazy. Her focus on the fine line separating the committed artist from the 'committed' lunatic is a direct challenge to the ease of integration of much so- called critical art. She actively asserts the necessity of marginality and danger. The extremity of her stance causes one to wonder if going on stage and smearing chocolate on one's nude body may be a cop-out for both artist and voyeur. (Rose, 1993: 101)

Orlan also draws attention to the limits of the artist's body, and to how it might be extended. As an anti-celebrity she nonetheless draws attention to the death that will eventually become us all.

Immortality

Celebrity status grants one symbolic immortality; one's name, one's image, one's activities and art get written into history books, artistic canons, and are carried across time and space, so that the famous figure lives on, way beyond the telos of the body. Virtual and digital stars do this living forever in a different way; with no mortal body to speak of, they cannot physically die, and so they live on without mourning or funeral, only beholden to archiving strategies and continued public interest in them. Their images float in virtual clouds that are eternally blessed. Higher order celebrities are already post-human, Divine: they have gone beyond the mortal limits of the body, and their immortality grants them religious signification.

Celebrities do something particular with ageing. On the one hand, they so readily embody the highs and lows, the inevitable trajectories of ageing, as we witness, first hand, bodily, physical transformations. As the celebrity gets old, as we grow older with them, they provide an avenue for age identification, for making sense of the ageing process, so we can deal with it, feel more secure or safe with it as our own bodies begin to change and fail us. This bardic mirror provides us with stability and holds the fear of ageing at bay. Of course, celebrities are allowed to age differently depending on their gender. Female celebrities grow old either as cougars and vamps, or as mothers and matriarchs; either as a red winter or a sunflower spring, reproducing gender binaries as they are forced to do so.

On the other hand, celebrities seem to arrest the signs and symptoms of ageing, be it through healthy living and pharmaceutical and cosmetic enhancement. A certain 'youthful' set of celebrity images can come to define them, so that they never seem to get old. Those celebrities who die young can never age; their youthfulness lives on forever. Celebrities can put us back in touch with our youth, they can provide the soundtrack, the images, the sensations to emotional memories first formed long ago and that we wish to return to, as we get old.

Celebrity culture is predominately youthful and young: the media is dominated by stories of the latest starlit, hunky action hero, pop star sensation, and sports hero. The images, sounds, and sensations they are attached to are youthful too: we see, hear, touch, smell, and taste them in the flowering of youth. Nonetheless, fans stay with, or true to, their primary celebrity identifications, a bond formed in youth but which often carries to the grave. This is another way to explain the metronome, as it draws youth and age, here/now and there/then, to connect us across the full breadth (breath) of a life to the beat, the beat, the beat of the metronome.

And what is my position in all this celebrity stuff, where do I stand? I stand divided, caught by its ideological and commercial ugliness, yet set free by its carnal callings and sensorial transgressions. I stand in the wake of celebrity's endless commodification streams, and its spectacle events that are light in substance, and yet I walk proudly in its undoubted ability to border cross, and raise political consciousness. I am occasionally ashamed by the pleasures it gives me, dependent as these are on a bourgeois individualism and a sickly romanticism, and yet I dance, dance, dance in its aesthetic beauty, and deeply touching and uplifting (transcendental) songs. Ultimately, the song, the beat of celebrity culture is one I am glad to hear and feel. I am a defender of what celebrity productively offers fans, and of the way it carries forward a sensuous knowledge that is not beholden to dominant ideology and semiotic power. Listening to Elvis Presley really did move my body; watching Georgie Best play sublime soccer really did anchor my experience of being Irish decent at the time of the Troubles; and I really do dream of being Leif Memphis, because I really am Leif Memphis...

Leif Memphis: whisky, concrete poetry, weed, and cherry blossoms. ...

Bibliography

Anon (2012) Katie Breaks Free, *US Weekly*, available at: http://www.usmagazine.com/celebrity-news/news/katie-holmes-felt-like-she-was-in-rosemarys-baby-with-tom-cruise-marriage-201227 (accessed 5 August 2012).

Anon (January 2012) Lydnsey, *Playboy Magazine* [United States].

Anon (2012) Richest Sportsmen in UK 2012 – Sunday Times Sport Rich List, *Sunday Times*, available at: http://www.therichest.com/sports/richest-sports-ment-in-uk-2012/ (accessed 6 May 2012).

Anon (2012) Singer Whitney Houston Dies at 48, *Fox News*, http://www.foxnews.com/entertainment/2012/02/11/whitney-houston-dies-at-48/) (accessed 6 April 2012).

Anon (2012) Walt Disney Co, *Reuters*, http://www.reuters.com/finance/stocks/companyProfile?symbol=DIS (accessed 1 June 2012)

Anon (2008) Rourke Didn't 'Care for' 'Wrestler' Script, *Entertainment News*, http://www.upi.com/Entertainment_News/2008/12/08/Rourke-didnt-care-for-Wrestler-script/UPI-68981228764682/ (accessed 6 April 2012).

Anon (2006) Kidman Crowned Hollywood's Highest-Paid Actress, *ABC News Online*, available at: http://www.abc.net.au/news/2006–11–30/kidman-crowned-hollywoods-highest-paid-actress/2142066 (accessed 12 September 2011).

Anon (2005) Silent Scientology Birth for Tom and Katie? *MSNBC Today*, available at: http://www.today.com/id/9620245/ns/today-today_Entertainment/t/silent-scientology-birth-tom-katie/#.Uh3hMhZ1pE (accesssed 11 February 2012).

Abrahams, Stephanie (2012) Behind the Hype: Can One Direction Save the Boy Band? *Time Entertainment*, http://entertainment.time.com/2012/04/06/behind-the-hype-can-one-direction-save-the-boy-band/ (accessed 4 May 2012).

Adams, Sarah (2012) The Media Industry: How It's Economic Structure Impacts Consumer Behaviour, at http://www.sportsbusinesssims.com/the-media-in-dustry-economic-structure.htm (accessed 5 August 2012).

Adorno, Theodore and Horkheimer, Max (1979) *Dialectic of Enlightenment*, trans. J. Cumming, London: Verso.

Ashe, D. D., Maltby, J., and McCutcheon, L. E. (2005) Are Celebrity-Worshippers More Prone to Narcissism? A Brief Report, *North American Journal of Psychology*, 7, 239–246.

Auslander, Philip (2006) *Performing Glam Rock: Gender and Theatricality in Popular Music*, Michigan: University of Michigan Press.

Bakhtin, Mikhail (1984) *Rabelais and His World*, trans. Helcne Iswolsky, Bloomington: Indiana University Press.

Bann, Stephen (1998) Three Images for Kristeva: From Bellini to Proust, *Parallax*, 4(3), 65–79.

Barthes, Roland (1982) *Camera Lucida: Reflections on Photography*, Hill and Wang.

Barthes, Roland (2007) The Face of Garbo, in Sean Redmond and Su Holmes (eds), *Stardom and Celebrity: A Reader*, London: Sage, 261–262.

Benedictus, Leo (2011) From Stephen Fry to Hugh Grant: The Rise of the Celebrity Activist, *The Guardian*, http://www.guardian.co.uk/theguardian/2011/apr/16/celebrity-activists-hugh-grant (accessed 16 April 2011).

Bennett, Andy (1999) Subcultures or Neo-Tribes? Rethinking the Relationship between Youth, Style and Musical Taste, *Sociology*, 33(3), 599–617.

Bennett, James (2011) *Television Personalities: Stardom and the Small Screen*, London: Routledge.

Bennett, Jane (2001) *The Enchantment of Modern Life: Attachments, Crossings, and Ethics*, New Jersey: Princeton University Press.

Berger, John (1972) *Ways of Seeing*, London: Penguin.

Berlant, Lauren (2012) In a Nutshell, *Rorotoko*, http://rorotoko.com/interview/20120605_berlant_lauren_on_cruel_optimism/ (accessed 5 June 2012).

Berlant, Lauren (2011) *Cruel Optimism*, Durham:Duke University Press.

Boorstin Daniel (1992) *The Image: A Guide to Pseudo-Events in America*, London: Vintage Press.

Braudy, Leo (1986) *The Frenzy of Renown – Fame and Its History*, Oxford: Oxford University Press.

Cashmore, Ellis (2010) Buying Beyonce, *Celebrity Studies*, 1(2), 135–150.

Cashmore, Ellis (2006) *Celebrity Culture*, London: Routledge.

Cashmore, Ellis (2004) *Beckham*, New York: John Wiley and Sons.

Caughie, John (1984) *Imaginary Social Worlds: A Cultural Approach*, Lincoln: University of Nebraska Press.

Chernin, Kim (1994) *The Obsession: Reflections on the Tyranny of Slenderness*, London: Harper.

Coleman-Bell, Ramona (2004) Droppin' It Like Its Hot: The Sporting Body of Serana Williams, in Su Holmes and Sean Redmond (eds), *Framing Celebrity: New Directions in Celebrity Culture*, London: Routledge, 195–206.

Collins, Sue (2001) 'E' Ticket To Nike Town, *Counterblast: E-Journal of Culture and Communication*, 1(1), (November).

Couldry, Nick (2003) *Media Rituals: A Critical Approach*, London: Routledge.

Csaszi, Lajos (2010) Broadening the Concept of Media Rituals: Tabloids as 'Low Holidays of Television', *Eastbound*, http://eastbound.eu/2010/csaszi (accessed 10 June 2012).

Dams, Tim (2011) How the Internet Created an Age of Rage, London: *The Guardian* (*The Observer*), http://www.guardian.co.uk/technology/2011/jul/24/internet-anonymity-trolling-tim-adams (accessed 25 July 2012).

Davies, Jude (2001) *Diana, A Cultural History: Gender, Race, Nation and the People's Princess*, London: Palgrave Macmillan.

Debord, Guy (1977) *The Society of the Spectacle*, in Fredy Perlman and Jon Supak, London: Black and Red.

Deleuze (1986) *Cinema 1: The Movement-Image*, Hugh Tomlinson and Barbara Habberjam (trans), Minnesota: Minnesota University Press.

Doty, Alexander (1993) *Making Things Perfectly Queer: Interpreting Mass Culture*, Minneapolis: University of Minnesota Press.

Dyer, Richard (1997) *White*, London: Routledge.

Dyer, Richard (1992) Don't Look Now: The Male Pin-Up, in John Caughie (ed.), *The Sexual Subject: A Screen Reader in Sexuality*, London: Routledge, 265–276.

Dyer, Richard (1987) *Heavenly Bodies: Film Stars and Society*, London: Macmillan.

Dyer, Richard (1982) Don't Look Now, *Screen*, 23(3/4), 61–73.

Ellis, John (1982) *Visible Fictions*, London: Routledge.

Evans, Jessica and Hall, Stuart (1999) *The Visual Culture Reader*, London: Routledge.

Feasey, Rebecca (2008) Reading Heat: The Meanings and Pleasures of Star Fashions and Celebrity Gossip, *Continuum: Journal of Media and Cultural Studies*, 22(5), 687–699.

Foster, Eric (2004) Research on Gossip: Taxonomy, Methods, and Future Directions, *Review of General Psychology*, 8, 78–99.

Foucault, Michelle (1990) *The History of Sexuality: An Introduction*, trans. Robert Hurley, New York: Vintage Books.

Foucault, Michel (1977) *Discipline and Punish: The Birth of the Prison*, New York: Random House.

Frith, Simon (1996) Music and Identity, in Stuart Hall and Paul du Gay (eds), *Questions in Cultural Identity*, London: Sage, 108–127.

Garland, Robert (2005) Celebrity in the Ancient World, *History Today*, 55(3), 24–30.

Gabler, Neal (2000) *Life: The Movie: How Entertainment Conquered Reality*, Vintage Press.

Gamson, Joshua (1994) *Claims to Fame: Celebrity in Contemporary America*, University of California Press.

Gitlin, Todd (1997) *The Whole World is Watching: Mass Media in the Making and Unmaking of the New Left*, California: University of California Press.

Geraghty, Christine (2007) Re-Examining Stardom: Questions of Texts, Bodies, and Performance, in Sean Redmond and Su Holmes (eds), *Stardom and Celebrity: A Reader*, London: Sage, 99–110.

Goodman, Mike and Barnes, Christine (2010) Star/Poverty Space: The Making of the Development Celebrity, *Environment, Politics and Development Working Paper Series Department of Geography*, King's College London, Paper #35.

Hall, Stuart (2013) The Kilburn Manifesto: Our Challenge to the Neoliberal Victory, *The Guardian*, http://www.guardian.co.uk/commentisfree/2013/apr/24/kilburn-manifesto-challenge-neoliberal-victory (accessed 25 April 2013).

Hanlon, Karen (2006) Heavy Metal Carnival and Dis-Alienation: The Politics of Grotesque Realism, *Symbolic Interaction*, 29(1), 33–48.

Harper, Stephen (2006) Madly Famous: Narratives of Mental Illness in Celebrity Culture, in Su Holmes and Sean Redmond (eds), *Framing Celebrity: New Directions in Celebrity Culture*, London: Routledge, 311–328.

Hermes, Joke (1995) *Reading Womens Magazines: An Analysis of Everyday Media Use*, London: Polity.

Hartley, John (1999) *Uses of Television*, London and New York: Routledge.

Hills, Matt (2002) *Fan Cultures*, London: Routledge.

Hollander, Paul (2011) Celebrities, 'Extravagant Expectations' and the Love Life of Americans, http://rowmanblog.typepad.com/rowman/2011/06/celebrities-extravagant-expectations-and-the-love-life-of-americans.html (accessed 8 January 2012).

Holmes, Su and Redmond, Sean (2006) *Framing Celebrity: New Directions in Celebrity Culture*, London: Routledge.

Inglis, Fred (2010) *A Short History of Celebrity*, Princeton University Press.

Jenkins, Henry (2010) Fandom, Participatory Culture, and Web 2.0 – a Syllabus, *Confessions of an Aca-Fan*, http://henryjenkins.org/2010/01/fandom_participatory_culture_a.html (accessed 11 June 2011)

Jenkins, Henry (2007) Transmedia Storytelling 101, *Confessions of an Aca-Fan*, http://henryjenkins.org/2007/03/transmedia_storytelling_101.html (accessed 1 February 2011).

Jenkins, Henry (2006) When Fandom Goes Mainstream, *Confessions of an Aca-Fan*, http://henryjenkins.org/2006/11/when_fandom_goes_mainstream.html (accessed 1 February 2011).

Jenkins, Henry (1996) Fandom, the New Identity Politics, *Harper's Magazine*, 23–24 June.

Juslin, P. N. and Vastfjall, D. (2008) Emotional Responses to Music: The Need to Consider Underlying Mechanisms, *Behavioral and Brain Sciences*, 31(5), 559.

Kellner, Doug (2009) Barack Obama and Celebrity Spectacle, *International Journal of Communication*, 3, 715–741

Kellner, Doug (2003) *Media Spectacle*, London: Routledge.

Knee, Adam (2006) Celebrity Skins: The Illicit Textuality of the Celebrity Nude Magazine, in Su Holmes and Sean Redmond (eds), *Framing Celebrity: New Directions in Celebrity Culture*, London: Routledge, 161–176.

King, Barry (2008) Stardom, Celebrity and the Para-Confession, *Social Semiotics*, 18(2), 115–132.

Kuhn, Annette (2010) Memory Texts and Memory Work: Performances of Memory in and with Visual Media, *Memory Studies*, 3(4), 298–313.

Langer, John (1981) Television's Personality System, *Media, Culture, and Society*, 3(4), 351–365.

Llewellyn-Smith, Casper (2002) *Poplife: A Journey by Sofa*, London: Sceptre.

Little, Michael (2004) Pure Professionalism: A Man Made Picture (Thoughts on Collateral), *The Film Journal*, http://www.thefilmjournal.com/issue9/collateral2.html (accessed 1 August 2011).

Liza Tsaliki, Christos A. Frangonikolopoulos and Asteris Huliaras (2011) *Transnational Celebrity Activism in Global Politics*, Chicago: The University Chicago Press.

Lowe, Melanie (2003) Colliding Feminisms: Britney Spears, 'Tweens', and the Politics of Reception, *Popular Music and Society*, 26, 123–140.

Lowenthal, Leo (1961) *Literature, Popular Culture, and Society*, Englewood Cliffs, NJ: Prentice-Hall.

Lutz, Catherine and Collins, Jane (1994) *The Photograph as an Intersection of Gazes: The Example of National Geographic*, London: Routledge.

Maltby, John, Houran, J., Lange, R., Ashe, D., and McCutcheon, Lynn (2002) Thou Shalt Worship No Other Gods – Unless They Are Celebrities: The Relationship between Celebrity Worship and Religious Orientation, *Personality and Individual Differences*, 32, 1157–1172.

Maltby, J., Giles, D., Barber, L., and McCutcgheon, L. E. (2005) Intense-Personal Celebrity Worship and Body Image: Evidence of a Link Among Female Adolescents, *British Journal of Health Psychology*, 10, 17–32.

Maplesden, Allison (2012) *Toxic Celebrity* (unpublished PhD thesis, Deakin University).

Marks, Laura U. (2000) *The Skin of the Film: Intercultural Cinema, Embodiment and the Senses*, Durham: Duke University Press.

Marx, Karl (1981) *Capital: Volume 1: A Critique of Political Economy*, London and New York: Penguin Books.

Miller, Susan (2004) *Disgust: The Gatekeeper Emotion*, London: Routledge

Mulvey, Laura (1975) Visual Pleasure and Narrative Cinema, *Screen* 16.3, Autumn, 6–18.

Newman, George, Diesendrock, Gil, and Bloom, Paul (2011) Celebrity Contagion and the Value of Objects, *Journal of Consumer Research*, 38, 1–15.

Nokes, Tim (2011) Bad Girl Blues, *Social Stereotype*, available at: http://www.social-stereotype.com/_/Features/Entries/2011/7/27_LANA_DEL_REY.html (accessed 4 August 2012).

Nokes, Tim, (2011) Lana Del Rey: Bad Girl Blues, *Social Stereotype*, available at: http://www.socialstereotype.com/_/Features/Entries/2011/7/27_LANA_DEL_REY.html (accessed 22 March 2012).

North, Adrian and Hargreaves, David (1999) Music and Adolescent Identity, *Music Education Research*, 1(1), 75–92.

Orth, Maureen (2003) *The Importance of Being Famous: Behind the Scenes of the Celebrity-Industial Complex*, New York: Owl Books.

Payne, Tom (2010) *Fame: What the Classics Tell Us About Our Cult of Celebrity*, London: Picador.

Quinton, Matt (2012) Whitney Houston Found Dead at 48, *The Sun,* http://www.thesun.co.uk/sol/homepage/news/4124350/Whitney-Houston-found-dead-at-48.html (accessed 22 March).

Rojek, Chris (2001) *Celebrity*, Reaktion Books.

Rojek, Chris (2009) So You Wanna Be on Reality TV? *The Faster Times*, http://www. thefastertimes.com/fameculture/2009/09/03/no-talent-reality-tv/#more-23 (accessed 3 April 2012).

Rose, Barbara (1993) Orlan: Is It Art? Orlan and the Transgressive Act, *Art in America*, 81(2), 83–125.

Redmond, Sean (2010) Avatar Obama in the Age of Liquid Celebrity, *Celebrity Studies*, 1(1), 81–95.

Redmond, Sean (2011) Pieces of Me: Celebrity Confessional Carnality, in Sean Redmond (ed.), *The Star and Celebrity Confessional*, London: Routledge, 41–53.

Redmond, Sean (2008) When Planes Fall Out of the Sky, in Karen Randell and Sean Redmond (eds), *The War Body on Screen*, New York: Continuum.

Redmond, Sean (2006) Intimate Fame Everywhere, in Su Holmes and Sean Redmond (eds), *Framing Celebrity: New Directions in Celebrity Culture*, London: Routledge, 27–44.

Rein, Irving, Kotler, Philip, and Stoller, Martin (1997) *High Visibility: The Making and Marketing of Professionals into Celebrities*, New York: McGraw-Hill.

Rintoul, Suzanne (2004) Loving the Alien, Ziggy Stardust and Self-Conscious Celebrity, *M/C Journal*, 7(5), November, http://journal.media-culture.org. au/0411/03-rintoul.php (accessed 6 May 2011).

Rockwell, Donna and Giles David C., (2009) Being A Celebrity: A Phenomenology of Fame, *Journal of Phenomenological Psychology*, 40, 178–210.

Rowland, Mark (2008) *Fame*, London: Acumen Publishing.

Rubin, A. M., Perse, E. M., and Powell, R. A. (1985) Loneliness, Parasocial Interaction, and Local Television News Viewing, *Human Communication Research*, 12, 155–180.

Saunders, Rhonda (1998) The Legal Perspective on Stalking, in J. Reid Meloy (ed.), *The Psychology of Stalking: Clinical and Forensic Perspectives*, London: Academic Press, 28–51.

Sconce, Jeffry (1995) Trashing the Academy: Taste, Excess and an Emerging Politics of Cinematic Style, *Screen*, 36(4) (Winter), 371–393.

Sobchack, Vivian (2004) *Carnal Thoughts: Embodiment and Moving Image Culture*, California: University of California Press.

Sobchack, Vivian (2000) What My Fingers Knew: The Cinesthetic Subject, or Vision in the Flesh, *Senses of Cinema*, 5, April, http://sensesofcinema. com/2000/5/fingers/ (accessed 1 February 2011).

Soukup, Charles (2006) Hitching a Ride on a Star: Celebrity, Fandom, and Identification on the World Wide Web, *Southern Communication Journal*, 71(4), 319–337.

Storey, John (2001) *An Introduction to Cultural Theory and Popular Culture*, London: Pearson.

Squire, Corinne (1994) Empowering Women? the Oprah Winfrey Show, in Kum-Kum Bhavnani and Ann Phoenix, *Shifting Identities, Shifting Racisms: A Feminism and Psychology Reader*, London: Sage, 63–79.

Stacey, Jackie (1994) *Star Gazing: Hollywood Cinema and Female Spectatorship*, London: Routledge.

Totaro, Donato (2002) Deleuzian Film Analysis: The Skin of the Film, *Off-Screen*, http://www.horschamp.qc.ca/new_offscreen/skin.html (accessed 1 August 2011).

Tuite, Claire (2007) Tainted Love and Romantic Literary Celebrity, *ELH*, 74(1), Spring, 59–88.

Turner, Graeme (2010) *Ordinary People and the Media: the Demotic Turn*, London: Sage.

Turner, Graeme (2006) The Mass Production of Celebrity: Celetoids, Reality TV, and the Demotic Turn, *International Journal of Cultural Studies*, 9(2), 153–165.

Turner, Graeme (2004) *Understanding Celebrity*, London: Sage.

Turner, Graeme, Bonner, Frances, and Marshall David, P. (2000) *Fame Games: The Production of Celebrity in Australia*, Cambridge: Cambridge University Press.

Tsaliki, Lisa, Frangonikolopoulos, Christos, A., and Huliaras, Asteris (2011) *Transnational Celebrity Activism in Global Politics: Changing the World?* Bristol: Intellect.

Thrift, Nigel (2008) *Non-Representational Theory: Space, Politics, Affect*, London: Routledge.

Vernon, Polly (2007) I Didn't Like Being a Celebrity. It's a Service Job. Like Washing Toilets, *The Observer*, 8 July, http://www.guardian.co.uk/music/2007/jul/08/popandrock2 (accessed 12 November 2012)

Wang, Yiman (2007) A Star Is Dead: A Legend Is Born: Practising Leslie Cheung's Posthumous Fandom, in Sean Redmond and Su Holmes (ed.), *Stardom and Celebrity: A Reader*, London: Sage, 326–340.

Weber, Brenda (2009) *Makeover TV: Selfhood, Citizenship, and Celebrity*, Durham: Duke University Press.

Wettach, Gabriel (2011) For the Love of Jodie Foster: Star Demystification and National Configuration, in Sean Redmond (ed.), *The Star and Celebrity Confessional*, London: Routledge, 96–112.

Wilson Julia, A. (2010) Star Testing: The Emerging Politics of Celebrity Gossip, *The Velvet Light Trap*, 65, Spring, 25–38.

Wood, Sam Taylor (2004) New Work Exhibition, 28 October – 4 December, White Cube Hoxton Square, London.

Index